On Being a Man

Four Scottish Men in Conversation

*To Judith
Hope you enjoy a wee
bit d controversy!
Sandy
25/8/14*

**SANDY CAMPBELL, JOHN CARNOCHAN
PETE SEAMAN and DAVID TORRANCE**

Luath Press Limited
EDINBURGH
www.luath.co.uk

First published 2014

ISBN: 978-1-910021-33-0

The paper used in this book is recyclable. It is made from
low chlorine pulps produced in a low energy, low emissions manner
from renewable forests.

Printed and bound by
Bell & Bain Ltd., Glasgow

Typeset in 11 point Sabon
by 3btype.com

Contents

Scottish Men are Everywhere and Nowhere

GERRY HASSAN

MEN ARE EVERYWHERE in Scotland. Talking in positions of power, being loud and noisy in public life, organisations and public spaces.

Yet, amid this noise, there is also a deafening silence, one so powerful that many do not even notice or comment on it, instead seeing it as the natural state of affairs. This silence is of men not talking and being reflective of what it is to be a man.

This book enters into what are, still, in Scotland, uncharted waters by venturing onto the terrain of men talking and engaging as men. It does not aim or claim to cover everything. It is offered as a start and an opening: an invitation to aid and encourage future conversations and considerations about some of the most important issues facing Scotland.

The four men who are involved in this – Sandy Campbell, John Carnochan, Pete Seaman and David Torrance – are not claiming to, or being put up to, speak for all Scottish men. That would be both problematic and counter-productive. Nor are they claiming to represent the different varieties of Scottish men and masculinities. Men across Scotland come in all sorts and types: with a wide spectrum of backgrounds, lives, interests, identities, voices and accents.

The gang of four gathered in this book are all middle class and white. But there are important and revealing differentiations between them. They are aged between 36 and 61 years old, spanning at least a generation. Three are Scots born and one English born, and one of the Scots born has spent a large part of his adult life in England. There are differences in sexuality, and a variety of political persuasions. In the latter, these range from those who have identified with the centre-left and nationalists, to a more sceptical take on Scotland's progressive credentials.

Looking at the four by their professional careers and chosen work, two have chosen to work in challenging areas which have male behaviour and role models at their essence – police and, in particular, the issue of violence (John) and apprenticeships and how boys become men (Sandy). The remaining two have worked in policy research specialising in public health (Pete) and media and commentary (David). The four are thus a mix of talkers and contemplators, and do-ers, thereby combining those looking for the big picture or pattern, and those trying to aid social and cultural change.

One of the main motivations behind this book is the belief, which I agree with firmly, of all four who took part in these exchanges, that the silences and evasions of too many men in our society contribute to and magnify the problems we face in relation to individual and collective behaviour.

A central strand running through the book and discussions is how do men take responsibility, what should they act on, speak on, and challenge other men on? The conversations range far and wide, starting with a series of autobiographical introductions in which each of the men in turn reflect on their backgrounds, upbringings and how they became the men they are today.

From this, the conversations address some of the key issues of society and men: the violence men do to other men and themselves, the dramatically altering world of work and employment, how male role models have altered profoundly in a generation, and the importance and influence of our fathers and mothers, and how we bring up our children. They talk and reflect on the changing relationships of men and women in society, in work and as partners.

They get into areas which are difficult, ambiguous and often not heard in public. They admit doubts, fears and anxieties, as well as talking about the power of love and the need for empathy. At points they express anger and frustration, or even incomprehension, not claiming to have all the answers.

One tone which emerges amongst the many is that of loss. By this I mean loss of past worlds of supposed certainties, where we are led to believe it was somehow simpler to be a man and express masculine traits. This lost world – of traditional industries and often gruelling and demanding work produced a culture of what some call 'big men' – but which was a mosaic of many different types of men, including that of working class self-educated, politically literate men.

There was no 'golden age' in any of this, yet its passing has led in some places to a lament for the importance it put on a certain version of masculinity. The exchanges on this reflect on the different nuances of that loss, and the world that has emerged in its place: a sense of elegy, but also exploration, of what this all amounts to as a new generation grows up, compared to their dads and grandfathers.

The debate about the roles, views and behaviours of men in Scotland cannot be seen as a marginal one, or a sideshow to the real business: politics or jobs and the economy. All of these areas and more – work, how we raise and support children, looking after aging relatives, the nature of public sector employment, and the realities of a decade of Tory inspired austerity, all have a gender dimension.

None of this can be ignored, left in silence or subsumed in what are meant to be 'bigger' political issues. For too long, parts of Scotland have got away with arguing that these real live issues have to be relegated below the important subjects, whether it is the Left's view of the world or the national question. It is a little wonder that Scotland has a gender gap in how it does politics or how independence is seen, for until these areas tackle the thorny, complicated issues of how men and women live together better, then these will seem less real and connected to many people.

This means that men need to start speaking up as men, changing themselves and challenging other men to take responsibility. This means taking risks, not only by being brave and bold, but also admitting insecurities and vulnerabilities. It means having no 'no-go areas' of debate in Scottish society, and demanding that men talk about their roles, hopes and fears, and the gender dimensions of so much of Scottish society.

This book is a contribution to starting that. It does not claim to have the final word on everything or indeed anything, but where there was once silence, there is now the prospect of the beginning of a debate.

For taking those brave steps, I want to thank Sandy, John, Pete and David, for being prepared to give their time and views in this fascinating and important set of exchanges. It has been long overdue. Now we have an opportunity to use their reflections to facilitate a wider and much needed debate about Scottish men.

Gerry Hassan
May 2014

CHAPTER ONE

Introductions and Personal Stories

PETE SEAMAN

I GREW UP IN a place called the Wirral. My early years feel inseparable from the geography of an unremarkable place which, undergoing the seismic shifts the 1970s and 1980s brought, defined my particular sense of normal. Perhaps it is also a particularly male place to start, on a map rather than in the expressive warmth of a home or relationships, but I will come to those later.

The Wirral usually needs some explanation for people who have not spent time there. Located in the North West of England it is defined by its neighbours. Through either of the Mersey tunnels sits the more recognisable city of Liverpool and to the south east the county of Cheshire. The Wirral exists between these two relatives with its affiliation in confusion. I grew up in a town that seemed to capture the uncertainty of this place, a new build overspill of homes affordable to skilled manual workers employed in car plants or light engineering. In those days it would require one income, usually the male one, to pay the mortgage (£5,000 for the home I grew up in). Today, it is more likely to require two. Then, it offered young couples somewhere green, clean and beyond the expectations of their own parents.

In this place you were never sure of whom you were. You were neither 'from' Liverpool nor *not* from there. 'Over the water', Liverpudlians fiercely defended the gates of who was in and out of the Scouser club. Lads growing up on the Wirral wanted to be in it but weren't allowed. We were 'plastic Scousers'. My father was a proud Liverpudlian who never quite adapted to life over the water and the future it represented. He was a precision engineer who caught the downward trajectory of Merseyside's manufacturing base. His father owned an engineering firm when local engineers built the world. My dad became self-employed as the docks and heavy engineering that fed the smaller firms began to struggle and collapse. 'Never get into engineering' he solemnly told me (the only career advice I ever received). I saw his hands every day with fingerprints etched out in black, and his clothes smelt of something we all knew as 'solly oil'. Curled shards of metal ('swarf' – the fact that I have to put these words in quotes shows the distance between our working worlds) were pressed into every shoe he owned. I overheard stories of horrific accidents, usually involving eyes and fingers. I remember the orchestra of lathes, mechanical saws and other machinery producing an unceasing rhythmic pounding my brother believes caused my dad's current dementia. Not a standard medical opinion but when I heard that Lou Reed produced an avant garde record called *metal machine music* to get out of a record contract, I had a fair idea of what it might have sounded like. My dad worked hard for little reward, he was swimming against an economic and political tide. His experience and those of many other men he knew has left me with a sense of never being able to take our livelihoods for granted, not just our jobs but the entire sectors we work in.

The map my dad inherited didn't fit the post-industrial landscape he found himself in. Elements of the 1980s seemed alien to him. His sons appeared molly coddled at home and school, with posters on their bedroom walls of men with striking haircuts. At least the football offered a masculinity he could recognise. My dad, my brother and I bonded over football. It offered a link we could all understand to the old city that shaped him. First sitting in the stands and then, we when he felt we were old enough, introduced to 'the parapet', our particular inherited corner of the famous Kop. It was unspoken that the things we did and witnessed there, the flouting of suburban standards of hygiene, health, safety and decorum, would not be reported when we returned home. The lines of men taking a piss against the back wall of the stand and the resulting waterfall down the terrace. The excitement of a crowd surge lifting you off your feet and depositing you yards from where you started. We would shout ourselves hoarse in support of men from Scotland, Ireland, Wales and Scandinavia. Not a Scouser amongst them but they had a commitment to the people who watched them that still moves me. It felt like the Kop had been there forever, a fixed reference point across generations, that I might have believed could never vanish.

The Kop's loss of first its innocence, and then of its recognisable physical form, was perhaps the only one of my father's bereavements I could understand and share. Not that we talked about such things. The day after Heysel I remember him asking me to change out of my Liverpool T-shirt before going out to play. The night before, he had taken no interest in the game. A small argument took place that summer between my parents about the appropriateness of my brother taking a Liverpool kit on holiday to Italy. Our making friends with two Italian boys in the resort seemed to bring peace to both of them. I don't remember how or if we spoke about Hillsborough. It is my mum I remember then. The only time I remember her at the ground was a fine summer's evening when we stood silent looking toward the flower decked terrace. The last time I remember the four of us going somewhere together. There were tears but we didn't have the skills in our family to talk about this. Perhaps no one did back then. We were all beginning to feel a bit lost. My dad's dismissive one-liners to describe just about any category of person or event were useless in explaining something of this magnitude. So was his lexicon of 1950s Liverpool, full of words such as 'spinster', 'bachelor', 'nesh', 'clown', 'cack-handed'. Words used neutrally but had such a damning, definitive quality to them they made me flinch. Words people could never recover from.

My mum represented the future, much more comfortable in both her suburban surroundings and the times. She was the opposite of my dad: sociable, talkative, outgoing, expressive, and open. She was the one I wanted to be like. The one whose sense of right and wrong was the one I would try to live by. She ran the youth club and taught school leavers at the local technical college, both roles giving her the genuine love of count-less teenagers. Seriously, being my mum's son got me respect and credit I scarcely deserved. Word was she was 'sound'. Whereas my dad closed off to the problems the 1980s brought, my mum faced them head on. She wanted to go to Greenham Common but didn't want to leave two young boys in the care of my dad ('why didn't you just take us!' me and my brother cried when we heard, sorry to have missed out). At one point she wanted us all to go and live on a commune but then thought we would be better carrying on at school. We marched for miners and stood in vigil for John Lennon. My mum was on TV when a school closed by the council was re-opened by volunteers. My dad was a socialist too but my mum had more hope, believing in everyone's inherent humanity and that one day soon, good would prevail. My dad was being ground down. His liveli-hood, the one he had not chosen but was given to him, was becoming something men used to do.

My dad left home when I was 17 on a sunny day after school. I remember he left us a five pound card for the electricity meter. Confusingly, typically, this was both thoughtful and misjudged. I felt a sense of relief. Not that he had gone but that it had finally happened. I grew in my dad's absence. Not that he was in anyway abusive but his presence had a way of making me feel awkward about who I was and who was becoming. My mum worked hard to keep the roof over our head. I was proud of what she was doing and of being a single parent household. But my mum was devastated by the betrayal 'your father' (as she could only ever describe him) represented. Alcohol became more and more ubiquitous. My dad's increasing emotional distance actually made it easier for me when he did leave. For many years after, I suppressed elements of my personality I felt were inherited from him or were like him. I wanted to do masculinity in a way different from him, if I was going to have to do it all. The irony is that now my dad, with severe dementia, possesses a sense of vulnerability he can accept, he is coming to terms with his own fallibility. Now, I would be happy to be like him.

SANDY CAMPBELL

When I think of introducing myself as a writer about Scottish men or manhood, I waver. Not because of any false modesty; nor for any inverted feminist or quasi-internationalist excuse. I am a proud male and a proud Scot, but here's the rub: am I Scottish and male enough, and what's more – in equal doses?

Can you imagine that kind of conundrum on the female side? (Am I female enough? As if...) Maleness seems to demand certainty. So does Scottish-ness for that matter. I've always believed that male identity is strangely fragile alongside female identity. A bit of 'bum fluff' on your upper lip and unpredictable pitch in your teens, but with girls, they physically and visually change into women! No question about it.

On the nationality thing, what does it mean to be Scots? Maybe you just kinda know it when you've got it. I've known it consciously since I was ten. My dad was swept up by the SNP in 1966. I was too. Winnie Ewing won Hamilton and I won the school mock election for the SNP, all in the same year. Unusual behaviour for a boy of that age, I know. I did other things too, like wedding myself fatefully to lifelong raised hopes and disappointment; namely being cursed with supporting Hibs.

Scottishness and maleness. They seem to sit together in some archetypal way. I think of the kilted Scottish soldier – with his white spats and glengarry. Who could be more male – and who more like a strutting peacock? A skirt as a national emblem, yet the women seem to love a man in a kilt.

But really my claim to speak on Scotland with any authority is mixed. I left Scotland for England-Yorkshire when I was aged 17 and didn't come back until I was 43 – in the year of the reconvened Scottish Parliament. It is now fifteen years on. My knowledge of Scotland, apart from in my soul, is either post-devolution or drawn from a childhood from the late '50s, '60s and early '70s. It's limited to South Edinburgh as a boy and Leith as a middle aged man. In between it was Yorkshire.

So, Yorkshire it was for the next quarter century. That makes me some kind of Anglo-Scot, or maybe now a 'Scots-Returnee'. I admire Alex Ferguson on many levels and his recent pronouncements on being Scots in England are worth a listen. He's one of the few Unionists that make me stop and think. Like thousands and thousands of Scots, I, too, made England my home and was happy there.

What does it mean to introduce yourself anyway? Apparently when North American Indians (they called them that in my boyhood) do so, they describe themselves by going back eight generations. For me, part of becoming a man is paying due respect to your elders and family ancestors. I continue to be surprised by how many people quite casually declare that they don't know anything of their grandparents. Sad how irrelevant the past has become to so many of us.

My dad, James Valentine Campbell, was Scots to his core – back to the dawning of time. There were McPhersons, Camerons and Andersons in the family tree. My dad was the youngest of eight and became a third generation painter and decorator along with most of his brothers. We used to joke about it being paint, not blood, in the Campbell family veins. I was named after my grandfather – Alexander. My grandmother, the daughter of a cobbler orphan from Deeside, was the only one of my grandparents still alive when I was born.

My mum, Perla, was a different kettle of fish. Born in Edinburgh, but of Anglo-Argentine stock, her parents were married in Buenos Aires in 1910. An unlikely match was the family wisdom. My grandmother was second generation Argentine, descending from the Scots and Welsh who went out in the mid 19th century to build the railways. In her 20s, whilst performing missionary work amongst the Guarani Indians of Paraguay, she met my grandfather. He was a Cockney adventurer 15 years her elder – an actual cowboy no less, but when he started trading in Guarani Indian silverware it all went wrong. Fast forward through their return to the UK, the shame of bankruptcy and the birth of my mum. He died when she was seven and the family got by thanks to money and parcels from back home – the Argentine.

Stories from before I was born but as an only child they had huge impact. Just five years ago I visited my Argentine relatives for the first time. Impossible to explain but it truly felt like a completion of a circle stretching back generations. This was the family that had stood behind my mum. But for quirks of fate my mum would never have left Buenos Aires; never met my dad; and never have produced me. I know the same goes for everyone but it doesn't stop it being a profound and humbling moment.

Then, on the sixth day of Christmas 1955, I enter the world – 'from my mother's womb untimely ripped'. My mum was 41. My dad was 42. They had met on outings of the Edinburgh Sketching Club in the years after the war. Two souls who thought their chances of married life, indeed parenthood, had gone. My dad had done okay for himself after being de-mobbed. Decorators were busy as post-war Edinburgh painted itself back together again.

They scrimped and saved and bought a dry rot-ridden house near the Meadows, and with my dad's skills, turned it into a very well presented middle class family home. My dad worked six days a week and we had summer holidays in Peebles or North Berwick. They chose to send me to a fee paying grant-aided school, which came to an end when the Heath Tory government gave schools like mine the ultimate choice: charge the full fees or join the state sector. Needless to say mine, Daniel Stewarts, was never in any doubt that full public school status was in their stars. That was when I left.

I had a mixed childhood emotionally. I have happy memories, but I remember a lot of sadness too. I felt the loneliness of being an only child with most of my class mates living on the other side of the city. I remember the shock of landing as an 'adolescent' and the whole struggle of those teenage years. I remember it suddenly coming together when I was 16 and then I remember a year later, when on 3 September 1973, I propelled myself into the adult world on the 11 o'clock south from Waverley – destination Yorkshire.

I left Auld Reekie in the early '70s to do a nine month work placement as a junior care assistant in a Dr Barnardo's home for disabled kids near Harrogate. I was paid £3 a week plus board and lodgings. I loved it. In Working Rite, the charity I set up and now run, we say 'everyone remembers their first boss'. Well mine was a woman, Margaret Frost, 13 years my senior, and really quite a force.

The 'kids' I was supposed to be looking after were just a year or two younger than me. They had spina bifida and muscular dystrophy, and it was the muscular dystrophy guys (Adrian, Robert – also known as Stan, and Stephen) who became good and close mates. I bathed, toileted and dressed them for nearly three years. Then one by one they died; bitter sweet years.

I may well have been young and in deepest Yorkshire, but nevertheless I left no one in any doubt that Scotland was where I came from. It was the early '70s. Jobs were a plenty and I went through a few. I particularly remember as a bus conductor on the run from Doncaster to Sheffield one summer morning, meeting the city that was to become home for the next 20 years. Sparks to the left, fiery molten metal to the right. A world that is now well gone but there I was standing awestruck beside the driver as our double decker confidently cruised through the Attercliffe steel works on the final run into Pond Street bus station. Upright proud and purposeful South Yorkshiremen became my role models as I groped my way into manhood.

I remember a National Union of Public Employees (NUPE) trade union official who took me under his wing – Ken Curran. He had more effect on the path of my life than he could ever realise. I remember my years as a gardener. Those guys knocked the edges off me in a really sound way. I was fit and I had fun. For three years not a day went by without laughing until my belly hurt.

And I remember that politics was never far behind and it was these passions that brought me ultimately into the centre of the early '80s Labour v Thatcherite struggles. As an eager and confident young trade unionist I got a job of a lifetime right in the middle of the miners' strike: as a professional political campaigner and assistant to a man who was for me in my late 20s and early 30s, an inspiration to work for – David Blunkett.

I remember, too, the Falklands War (which of course touched a certain Argentine nerve) and I remember my mum's sudden death spookily just after the Argentine surrender. And I remember my clumsy attempts in the years to come to reach out to my dad in some way at a distance of 300 miles when we were both paralysed by grief.

But what I don't remember, because I wasn't here, was the nationalist emergence in my homeland. I heard tales of this or that demo and a buzz over a pint on visits back home. But Orgreave and Hillsborough was my young adulthood. I settled into 'the dirty picture in a golden frame.' The Derbyshire peaks, watching the Blades, a good pint of Tetleys. Sheffield: it will never not feel like home. Yet return I did in 1998 and within a month I had settled in Leith.

What did I notice first about the Scotland I was reacquainting myself with? Well straight off it was how white the place was. No judgement; it was just weird after south Sheffield where it was split between traditional Yorkshire white working class, Punjabi-Kasmiris, African-Caribbean, and southern white settlers (who seemed to get most of the well paid jobs in the town hall). In Scotland most people seemed to be from the same tribe.

The other new small tribes seemed to be okay fitting in. The Sikhs in Leith were nothing like the Yorkshire Asians I remember. They were Scots, in such contrast to the way Sheffield Asians felt about not being English.

Then there was the casual violence. Perhaps that's too simple. It was more the unexpected nature of a very individual type of violence – or the threat thereof. Being physical just seemed to be more in the air. It wasn't a gang thing, it was just that the individual male seemed to take offence much easier than in Yorkshire – at least at that time. Yet the humour and the talkativeness and general gettin-on-with-each-ither-day-to-day was unmistakeable. There really did seem to be more of a community feeling around.

The next ten years was also the time of my dad. An American priest I much admire, Father Richard Rohr, uses the term 'Father Hunger'. It barely needs explanation, encapsulating as it does the yearning and loss felt by many men as they try to reach out to their dad.

Well, I was one of the lucky ones. Sadly, one of the very few. If there is anything to bring you face to face with yourself as a man it is the death of your father. From Winnie's speech at the opening Parliament in 1999, through to 2007 – the year of the first SNP administration, I was with him. There we were side by side in the SNP party by Edinburgh Castle on election night in 2007 when Alex Salmond came in as First Minister. My 93-year-old dad, a party member from before Hamilton, just joyfully couldn't believe it to the bottom of his soul.

The aging process is so central to any consideration of manhood. In my own view growing into manhood is almost as much about death as it is about life. How we pass, hopefully transform, into manhood from being and feeling like boys. How we flex ourselves and get things wrong on the way. How we pass through the decades and discover how little we actually do change.

I remember my young man's debates in the left wing maelstrom of the early '70s. Nurture versus nature. It was pretty clear, as a young socialist, which side I should come down on – the environment stupid! I shiver with embarrassment at the certainty we young lefties had. I've met way too many mums since who were themselves shaped by those new orthodoxies, and who then struggled hard to bring up their young boys without guns, only to roll their eyes in resigned surrender to the truth of nature.

They say there are three stages of man: in short trousers it's – 'my dad's better than your dad'. Then full of teenage righteousness we announce that actually our dad doesn't know anything about nothing. But for me I feel blessed to have tasted some of that last stage and find myself repeating the words: 'As my old dad used to say'.

JOHN CARNOCHAN

I was born in Motherwell in 1952. My parents were in their mid-40s when I was born and suspect I was unplanned, although never at any time felt unwelcome. I had two older brothers and an older sister. My sister is closest to me in age and she's ten years older and my oldest brother is 15 years older than me. This meant that by the time I was eight I was the only sibling still at home, it was like being an only child.

The family moved from Motherwell when I was about three to Wishaw, the neighbouring Lanarkshire town. My dad and my brothers worked in a local manufacturing firm that made railway wagons.

My dad did not have any hobbies that I recall, he didn't go to the football unlike almost every male at that time, although he did the pools coupon every week, we never won. Neither was he a regular attender at the pub, which for most of our neighbours was the weekly arrangement, men worked and went to the pub, women stayed at home and waited for their men. I do not recall going anywhere with my dad, just him and I, and we did not spend a lot of time together. We went on holidays but that was as a family. I didn't feel neglected by this lack of time with my dad but looking back I wish we had done some stuff together.

My dad had a strong sense of service and loyalty; I remember he used to give my brothers a hard time for being less than enthusiastic about their timekeeping. They worked together in the same factory but my dad was as a foreman and I suspect he had a hand in them getting jobs there, so perhaps felt they should not let him down. Every night my dad would polish his shoes and lay out his clothes for work the next day. He would never be late for anything. I'm like that too, iron a shirt, polish my shoes and lay everything out for work the night before and I hate being late for anything. He would always say that if you were washed, shaved and had a clean shirt and polished shoes you could go anywhere and meet with anyone. He always wanted me to join the police and when I eventually did in 1974 he was chuffed, he didn't actually tell me this but I heard it from other people.

My oldest brother went off to do his national service, I remember being very excited when he came back home on leave. He'd been stationed in Germany and drove a tank that seemed pretty cool to a six-year-old, who read Commando comics and had an arsenal of toy guns.

My dad got a job as chief of security at a whisky bond and bottling plant, there was a house with the job, so when I was seven we moved to another part of Lanarkshire. I went to a new school and made new friends. It was a very small school where three year groups shared just one teacher. I quite enjoyed school then, this would not last.

When I was bit older, early teens, I would go with the lorry drivers who worked out of the whisky bond to deliver cases of whisky to the docks in Glasgow. The practice of loading cargo into sealed metal containers which is used everywhere today was only just emerging then. Cardboard cases containing 12 bottles of whisky were loaded individually onto the back of flat-bed lorries and the load was then covered by a tarpaulin or hap and roped securely for the journey to the docks. There was of course a real technique to this whole process and it was also hard graft, so drivers always welcomed a second 'man' to help with the loading, roping and unloading and if the extra hands worked for just a few shillings even better. Delivering at the docks was always an exciting experience, ships docked there from all around the world.

The Vietnam War was in full swing at this time and the news always had a segment covering the most recent events in that war. It would be the taking of a town or a city, the Vietcong pushed back here or there, so many dead, and film clips of US fighter planes dropping napalm on forests which immediately caught light into a ferocious fire. It was all pretty one-sided, or so it appeared, I'd no idea of the notion of propaganda, I was just enthralled by the idea of men doing heroic things.

I recall too the improbable link I had to that war which involved whisky. The whisky that was blended and bottled at the plant was Cutty Sark which at the time was very popular in the US, so there were countless lorry loads of the stuff shipped to the troops fighting in Vietnam. Half gallon bottles of the Cutty Sark in cases with just two bottles being shipped off to destinations that I recognised from the news, with addresses stencilled onto the side of each case, US 3rd Airborne Calvary, Hanoi, US Marines 2nd Division, Phnom Peng. I remember thinking how strange that these men fighting a war that was portrayed as brutal against an enemy who were a dangerous and devious and had superior numbers yet they still had time for bevy.

Of the drivers I went with, one in particular impressed me, he had been in the parachute regiment, he never said much about this war in Vietnam but I always got the impression he was not particularly impressed by the US military. He predicted they would get beat.

I was now at secondary school and it was a real let down. I did not enjoy it and left as soon as I could, when I was 15. I can't really say exactly why I didn't enjoy school. The system of comprehensive education started about this time, so I sat an 11 plus exam and went to a high school and other friends went to a junior secondary.

The result was that none of the friends I hung around with either at primary school or where I stayed went to the same school as me; most of my friends were Roman Catholic and so went to their own school. Religion was never spoken of much in our house, none of my family supported a particular football team and all seemed quite relaxed about the whole sectarian issue. We lived in area where a lot of the families had direct and living relations from Ireland and I did know the words to a few Irish rebel songs which I learned from the guys I hung around with.

My parents always encouraged me to stay on at school but no one in our family or whom I knew went to university, so that wasn't ever a consideration. I had no particular ambitions career wise.

It was a time when getting a job was not so difficult and I had a few, some I lasted in for a few months some for a few weeks and one I remember was few hours, this was a bakery and I had to water down jam before squirting it into doughnuts, that's where I drew the line. Some of my friends worked in the steel works in Motherwell, Colvilles or Ravenscraig or Clyde Alloy. They made a lot of money for the time and for their age and spent it mostly on going out, there were dances in the local working men's clubs most weekends. I never really got into this scene. Drink made me ill and drunks bored me, both things still true today.

I met my wife when I was 16 and she was 15 and we have been together ever since. Hers was a Catholic family and so I had some work to do in convincing them that I was OK. I managed, eventually.

I joined the police in 1974 and got married the same year. I was 21. The police service at that time was not a well-paid job and my mates in the steel works earned as much as three times my salary. It was a secure job and it provided accommodation to married officers, which was the clincher. I found that I really enjoyed the work and I always did. I met some great people, I saw folk at their worst and their best, I learned not to take things too seriously and I learned that the two things my dad always prized, loyalty and service, were highly valued in the police.

DAVID TORRANCE

I grew up in Edinburgh, not in the leafy Georgian bit of the city everyone seems to envisage when they hear the name 'Edinburgh', but in a rather drab part of the Scottish capital just beyond the city centre. It was a bit of a mix. Lochend/Restalrig included a lot of what would still have been council-owned social housing when I was born in 1977, but there was also private housing, most of it rather modest.

My parents owned their own home, a semi-detached villa on a street called Marionville Drive. This makes it sound nicer than it was, although it was by no means unpleasant. But it was small. I shared a room with my (identical) twin brother for most of my childhood, before progressing to a hastily converted attic that was even smaller. As a teenager, I could only stand up to my full height in one part of the space.

I wouldn't say I had a particularly carefree childhood; certainly I don't look back on it with any of the nostalgia I detect when contemporaries of mine remember their (usually relatively well-heeled) early years. You'll detect an element of chippyness in that sentence and it's true, I'm quite chippy. I'm from a modest background and I'm reminded almost daily that whereas I've done relatively well in my career, I'm an exception rather than the rule.

My dad was from, if anything, a lower middle-class background. His father (though of humble origins) studied law at Edinburgh University after the war and became a solicitor in Edinburgh. His wife, my grandmother, was from a Borders family. Her father had been a station master both there and in Dunfermline. Visits to her house when I was a kid (my paternal grandfather died before I was born) were both tedious and a reminder that we weren't terribly well off.

My mum, on the other hand, was from a poor, working-class background. Her father was, among other things, a dustcart driver. I remember him playing his accordion (badly) during childhood visits. His wife, my maternal grandmother, was a very quiet, obviously decent woman who hadn't had (by the time she died in the mid-1980s) much of life beyond domestic chores (she lived in a tiny flat with her husband, five children and a cat).

Both my parents worked, my dad for the telecoms division of the General Post Office, later British Telecom. He built and maintained the green cabinets that litter the streets of Edinburgh and most towns and cities across the UK. My mum stopped working when my brother and I were born but returned when we were at primary school, first as a cleaner (NHS) and later as a typist doing secretarial work (latterly also with the NHS).

I was conscious as a child that we didn't have much money. There were few extravagances, and family holidays were to places like East Kilbride, Ayrshire and the south of Spain. Later, when my dad left BT to work in the private sector (also in telecoms), we had a bit more cash so made it over to the United States for several, much more enjoyable, holidays.

My dad was a relatively traditional Scottish male. He liked football (he was a season ticket holder at Easter Road), played golf, didn't like the Tories (he was and remains an SNP activist) and liked drinking, either at the SNP Club in Edinburgh or in various slightly dodgy city pubs. My mum was interested in none of those things. She hated sport, wasn't political (thus she voted Liberal) and didn't much like socialising.

My dad, God bless him, tried quite hard to introduce my brother and I to the joys of sport, if not Nationalist politics. He took us to Easter Road (I bloody hated it, so much noise) and bought us a set of junior golf clubs (I tried to look enthusiastic). But if my dad had visions of us regularly joining him on the football terraces and for leisurely rounds of golf, he must have been sorely disappointed.

My brother played along a little more convincingly than I did, but I just couldn't. A large part of it (for me) was because I'd realised by my mid-teenage years that I was gay and, as the journalist Matthew Parris once put it, one becomes gay to avoid things such as football. Unsurprisingly, I found myself detached from most normal male activity for someone of my background: women, beer drinking and sport.

They mystify me, to varying degrees, to this day, although I did develop a taste for beer a few years ago. It's fair to say that, as a result, my relationship (as a child) with my father wasn't particularly close. But that's changed over time. Although I still can't stand football, to me a peculiarly male obsession, I ended up accompanying my dad to games at Pittodrie when I was a student at Aberdeen.

I didn't enjoy them, of course, but I'd relaxed enough to derive some pleasure out of watching my father enjoy himself. The same was true when I took him to see the Proclaimers' musical, *Sunshine on Leith*, at the Festival Theatre in Edinburgh. We also have good-natured, though comically pointless, arguments about politics, although his desire for Scottish independence is another interest of his he failed to pass on to his offspring.

He's softened too, and occasionally I even detect pride in the modest achievements of his sons, although in professions and contexts that probably baffle him. Nevertheless, we've achieved some sort of balance, although this manifests itself in curious ways: he buys my books and I transfer engine parts on trips north to satisfy one of his other very male obsessions, tinkering with sports cars.

CHAPTER TWO

Work and Families

Dear Pete, John and David,

Here goes on 'Work'...

'Daddy's off to work.' One of the first phrases I understood. Even in times of high unemployment in the past – Daddy either worked or was looking for work. Then it changed, in our lifetimes. After hundreds, indeed arguably thousands of years, 'work' changed its gender pattern and assumptions.

The word 'work' is of course deceiving. In the main, women were not sitting with their heels up. In a recent article in *The Times* or *Telegraph* I read an excellent opinion piece reminding us of the time it once took to cook and clean a house and look after a family. I remember my mother's joy at the purchase of a twin tub. The hours that would be saved. Women worked bloody hard, but not where we did. Then after the twin tub my mum got a part time secretarial job.

Nevertheless, the 'three P's still carry resonance for me deep in my being: procreate, protect, provide. 'What do you do?' is another that trips off the tongue. Perhaps, despite its woolly language, a more accurate question, and meaning – what is your employment? What does someone pay you to do?

My first job was in a predominantly female environment. I was a care assistant. I remember my mother-in–law-to-be's pleasure at my becoming a bus conductor. A proper job for a man. Then a gardener. Even better. In seven years of running Working Rite we have placed over a thousand 16 to 18 year olds in full time six month work placements; over 60 per cent have been in construction trades. And in that time I can remember a girl plumber, a girl painter and now we have a girl brickie. But that's it. Boys and girls overwhelmingly want different jobs.

Is it wrong? No, I don't think so. Late teenagers are different by gender. Yes there's a growing minority that bucks the trend, and that's not wrong either, but there is something about a tool belt and hard boots that simply does it for a young male. Billy Elliot was a great film but I doubt there was not a sympathy from most of the audience for his dad's struggle at his son doing ballet, in the name of...!

From seeing countless teenagers in peer settings I see girls care, cooperate and bitch with each other in a way that boys simply don't. I remember a friend who was a primary school based counsellor. The kids had to put a request to see her into a box. Almost all the slips were from girls. Fall outs with friends, exclusions and cliques. Many sessions were needed. One day a slip appeared from two boys who had fallen out. The appointment time came and went so my friend went in search of them. They were found playing football in the playground. Back came the words from one of them: 'It's sorted miss!'

I would argue that a teenage boy needs to release a core male energy at that age – that manual work fulfils. Too much of our professionally designed educational activities don't suit boys. They are not meant to be penned into a classroom during daylight hours from 14 onwards. Now the barriers to career entry are melting away, girls' academic performance has been outstripping boys for more than a decade now. Try recruiting amongst the late '20s and early '30s these days and see the difference in calibre by gender. If I was allowed to advertise saying 'only females under 35 need apply' I would do it. It would save a lot of time and heartache being predictably disappointed with the quality of young men coming through.

Is it right that the ghettos of 'work' have radically changed? People of both genders and indeed the economy has benefitted. But with it has come a stifling cautiousness. I pen this whilst listen to Radio 3. In the break between pieces the commentator begins to make a point about the gender differences in who is playing what and how, but his comment peters off into the words 'I will probably offend too many people' and he stops in his tracks. Is that what we meant to do when we started out on this path of addressing the ills of patriarchy? Are we required to be gender blind to avoid making enemies? Have the new orthodoxies of the HR world tied our tongues and killed our humour? And what has happened to the quality of 'standing for something'?

I see more and more confident and sometimes angry women. I hear bizarre comments like 'we've made no progress.' Yet we still live in a world where gang rape haunts the buses of India and the Internet is groaning under the weight of traffic emitting degrading unspeakable abuse and humiliation of women. In another recent article I read of a mother's shock at hearing her teenage daughter tell her that she didn't like having oral sex with boys before going out with them – like all the others in her group!

What has happened to the qualities of chivalry and simply 'being your own man'? Purpose matters and learning the bravery to stand up to the power and danger of the male group. That was precisely the journey that young men were traditionally encouraged to make in various rites of passage. Now it seems the mantra is: cause no offence! If a man doesn't have a purpose (and work is such a natural setting for this) he is the poorer. In the not too distant past (and still sometimes now) these were qualities that were often learned in the workplace in late teenage years, handed down in the company of older men. It wasn't always ideal. There was cruelty sometimes but there were all sorts of men to witness over the years of an apprenticeship. Some you wouldn't want to follow in a month of Sundays. But others were naturally true mentors of the young.

Work is important to be a man. It has a unique male resonance. I make no apologies for that. For men it matters and without it, or if it's emasculating and pointless, it will eat away at a man's masculine soul. I find it no mystery that men are going under cover with the shadow side of their maleness. If that 'P' goes (to provide), and our role in procreation is up for question, and with the protect P being so tainted; what are we about? Because from being able to walk onwards – sticks and snails still have their genetic imprint.

All the very best,

Sandy

23 MARCH 2013

Dear John, Sandy and David,

As we alluded to in our introductions, our lifetimes have seen decline in forms of work traditionally associated with our gender. I wouldn't describe any of my paid jobs as being particularly 'male' jobs and all my 'proper' jobs have been in mixed environments and often predominantly female. As I remember them, my early jobs involved being paid to collect glasses in a pub, sweep-up in a factory, cook breakfasts in a hostel, serve baguettes whilst wearing a fetching cravat and give out phone numbers at a rate of one every 18 seconds. With the exception of the factory, these were all predominantly female environments and roles. In the all-male preserve of the factory, they had me doing 'lads' jobs which were supporting the 'real' work of the men – essentially cleaning up after them and going for their bacon rolls. None of these of course were my core identity defining activities at the time, done to get-by alongside the main business of completing interminable studies, usually in subjects in which the classes were predominantly female. I believed myself more suited to what I later learned where 'right brain' endeavours. Consequently, in my chosen occupation I've always found more women amongst my colleagues than men. My bosses, supervisors and managers have almost exclusively been female. So, what I know about 'masculinity' in work might be limited.

In part because of the extension of education from which I benefitted and in part because of the drive towards flexible employment practices when I entered work, I didn't have a 'proper' full-time job with any rights or protection until I was 28. This is an increasingly common experience now and I was reminded by reading Sandy's last contribution of how I entered full-time employment without much in the way of mentoring around the culture of work. What hasn't changed is Sandy's point that for my sense of who I am, work matters. Inwardly, I groan at my lack of imagination when asking a new acquaintance 'what do you do?' conscious of the import the answer has for people's self-esteem. Having a job, preferably in an occupation people will recognise is your mark of validation, that you are worth something and someone will pay you to do it.

The power of the three 'P's however, don't seem to have held for me. In my peer group the emphasis in work is on doing something socially valuable (or at least not damaging) and interesting. As I get older, I wonder if there is some narcissism at play here or perhaps adaptation to an economic reality; in a world of fixed-term contracts, procreating, protecting and providing feels like putting too much faith in continuity of employment. Liquid capitalism has made me a portable portfolio of skills with any roots laid-down achieved accidentally and retrospectively.

But what does this mean for how I enact my gender? Do I bring or construct 'maleness' about my work? In terms of qualities, a striving for independence may be an analogue of the historically masculine traits of instrumentality and efficacy. Independence of thought and deed and forging ones' own path which may have its origins in a male pioneer/loner spirit or a critical stance stemming from my Marxist gene (an uncomfortably masculine perspective, I've always felt). I am also aware of the contradiction. Marking one's self out in a competitive job market, left unchecked, can soon become a case of individual first, team player second.

Before entering the world of work, I judged the old model of masculinity a relic and saw this realisation as potentially liberating, rather than constraining. I had spent enough time chasing balls on school playing fields to know if I was to compete on my masculine traits I was destined for failure. Yet, the language I am choosing here of competitive games suggests my perspective to be more influenced by my gender than I realise. Unemployment remains my greatest fear. The ultimate defeat. Having experienced it temporarily, the denial of personhood it bestows is its abiding memory; the 'what do you do?' question at parties. Yet, it seems for men there are a shortage of alternative identities. The arguable progress which has been made for women in the workplace has not been matched by any great gains in men feeling a sense of worth and validity in adopting unpaid caring roles as a primary source of who they are. And I count myself amongst the intransigent.

As someone who saw opportunity and excitement in the blurring of gender boundaries, it is useful to be reminded of the young men Sandy meets, those who need to 'release core energy' for whom the controlled, unphysical nature of the classroom doesn't suit. Work in the weightless, post-industrial office or customer interface is unlikely to either. As Irvine Welsh put it 'If you liked school, you'll love work'. Yet I've heard women too complain of having to leave their personality at the door when going to their paid job. There's a sameness to many of today's working environments and the type of personality that succeeds within them. Who hasn't wondered how their colleagues' view of them would change if they met our longstanding friends of youth, our parents and siblings and knew the bizarre complexities of the clan? I can't help thinking class, rather than gender, is the thing. Where you come from matters less than where you are at or going. Are origins irrelevant in an equal opportunities environment if we're all the same? Leave difference at the door. But then, in Scotland at least, I've heard many preface an opinion or revelation with '*I'm from a working class background and...*' Back home (I still call it that!) the assumption of shared working class origins is so engrained to make its re-statement redundant.

To return to Sandy's crisis of masculinity in the workplace, I am taken by how the younger men in my work circles are comfortable with the new negotiation of gender and positively thrive within it. Post 1990s there's been the option of a knowing, ironic enactment of male gender stereotypes as a release valve to complement the five-a-side and rugged weekend pursuits. In reality, thes men do not want to put the clock back and welcome being able to ask colleagues what brand of tinted moisturiser gets them through the winter months (yes, I have been asked this and, confession time, I was able to recommend one). Of course, we are also middle class (born, or shaped by education). Which brings us to class again, is there a crisis of *working class* masculine identity being denied in contemporary work, part of the assault on this culture from the 1970s onwards?

I'm looking forward to hearing from John. The Police force strikes me as an institution that has had to change its culture rapidly since the dual forces of women increasing their representation at work and the homogenising influence of managerialism and risk awareness. Although, I admit to being informed by glib student politics and *Life on Mars* as to what the Police used to be like.

Best,

Pete

Dear Pete, Sandy and David,

Growing up in my family in the '50s and '60s, there was always an assumption that I'd work. I don't recall any definitive focus on a particular profession but getting a job and earning money was just assumed, similarly, getting married and having a family was just assumed. There was no shortage of jobs and therefore any man who didn't work was considered to be lazy. The general order of things was that men worked and this enabled men to earn money to find a wife, have a family and live. The type of job, the title of the job, the status that title inferred was irrelevant, it was about work. It was also true that women were unlikely to be in any way attracted to man who did not work. In many respects, successful family relationships were founded on this agreed mutuality.

My father and older brothers worked, and talk around the house during the week usually revolved around their work, about what would be on the sandwiches for work – 'the piece', was there any overtime to be had particularly Sunday working at double time and would this interfere with the weekend plans for going out. I listened to all this talk of working, earning and going out and waited for my turn at 15 to get involved.

My Mum didn't have a paid job outside the home until I was in my early teens and at secondary school. She was the one who ensured my father and brothers got to work on time, in clean clothes, well fed and ready to earn.

There was, for the overwhelming majority of people a very clear divide between the roles of men and women. This belief presumed that it was the men who worked and earned, they would marry women who had children and were supported by the men, who worked and earned. In our family all this work was viewed with respect and equal.

Men of the generation that preceded mine had fought in a war where their personal heroism, physical strength and masculinity were lauded. Their manly actions had saved the world and part of the legacy for me and the rest of my generation was a varied diet of books, films, stories and comics that recounted this masculine courage, celebrated it, glamourised it and perpetuated its fundamental importance to our collective well-being. 'We' had been fighting to protect a world that was now very quickly changing and I'm not sure ordinary men understood that, I don't believe my father and brothers did and neither do I think women did.

There had always been women working in vocations like nursing or teaching, as well as the more traditional type of 'women's work' in shops, secretarial and admin roles. These aside, I think that for the majority of women then the notion of work was not as a life-long career but rather to earn some money until marriage and family provided the opportunity to fill the roles of wife and mother full time. There was a growing movement for women's equality that was quite properly highlighting the gender inequalities that existed everywhere in society. That argument in relation to work roles increasingly portrayed the role of the woman who stayed at home to look after children and the home as being less worthy than the working role of men. I suspect that many women felt the pressure to have a job, later to become a career as well as being a wife and mother. So, rather than sharing the duties of work, home and child-rearing with men, women ended up doing everything, men were left to ask what their role was or indeed is.

The changing jobs market also played into this new horizon of equality fuelled by increasing consumerism and the need to 'own' things, so two wages were necessary to conform to all of society's expectations of the new family relationship.

The changing attitude to women's role and equality was accompanied by the decline of traditional industries where men's jobs were. I'm not sure which of these two different but connected social shifts had the most impact on the changing roles of men and women but together they altered the traditional view of men and women that my generation and countless other generations had been brought up with.

For many men the inability to 'provide' adequately for their family was source of personal failure and shame. Work was about providing for your family, the nature of the job was less important than actually being in a job and earning. Being a happily married man working to support your family is no longer considered a high tariff or creditable role in and of itself, similarly the role of being a 'house' wife looking after children and a home is not considered enough to fulfil the needs of a 21st century woman. We need to redefine work for men and women.

All the best,

John

Dear John, Sandy and David,

This morning I was having one of those chats about the sort of stuff we all do. Work, family, the weekend just passed. In the middle of the safe topics of socially acceptable male chit-chat; the giving a little bit but not too much, the skirting of the friendly but not over-familiar, something was said that perhaps crossed the boundary of safety. A doting, committed father told me about the time he was medically advised he was unable to have children. Having subsequently confounded medical opinion, it was how he spoke of his reaction to the diagnosis that stopped me; 'it was like being told I had failed as a man.' I didn't voice my thoughts but maybe my face gave me away; how do I feel about that statement? I am childless and at the time of writing and with no immediate plans to change the situation. Was it the potential to have children that completed his masculinity, or the act of raising them? What does his belief mean for my masculinity? How much do I care? These are questions I increasingly find myself having to find answers for as I go through a period of life in which other men I know are being fathers.

The idea of the female biological clock is well documented and represented in our culture. I first came across the subject among my friends around the age of 28. I remember it being exclusively a conversational concern initiated by my female friends. It took me by surprise when it was first raised as I barely felt a full adult yet myself. How could it have got this late so soon? Men have traditionally been considered immune to this growing urgency. But are we? If the amount of airtime it gets in conversation is anything to go by, perhaps we believe we are. Apparently, we are physically able to play our part in conception for more of our years and off the hook on the whole business of carrying and giving birth, but what about the other 18 plus years required to raise a child? It seems the window is vanishingly small between being 'responsibly' able to have children in terms of providing steady financial support *and* still having the energy and vigour to be an involved parent. I am always taken aback by parents of both genders who manage to have and raise children, provide for them, house them and still hold down stressful, relatively fast paced jobs. Particularly in the early years when children need so much attention. Some even have hobbies and a social life. How many hours do they have in their day? Does that mortgage not keep them awake at night?

Whilst this might make me lazy, does it make me less of a man? I'm not sure how to answer this. Of course I would like to claim it makes no difference but I'm not sure what my grounds are. My perception of the femininity or masculinity of my childless friends is undiminished by their choices or the fact they have not, yet, had children. Those who are fathers do not necessarily strike me as any more masculine. More responsible, perhaps. Blessed and lucky, definitely. I even notice my male friends are less traditionally masculine when around their children, giving them a freedom to express care and concern. They really seem to relish this aspect of their lives, it freeing them from the concerns of their public selves. I can then begin to see how it can be restorative experience to balance out the anxieties and fears that accompany such responsibility. I can also see how out of all the selves we present as we go through the world, this might be the one that captures them at their best.

A platonic female friend once challenged me after I spoke affectionately about a child we both know: 'Admit it, you want children don't you?' It felt like an impertinent question. Not the kind of question my male friends would ask me, not so directly. It is also not a question I ask of my childless male friends (about a 50/50 split between the parents and childless but this ratio is rapidly changing). And this is perhaps the interesting bit. Why do we not talk about our childlessness? Is it because the subject might be tinged with a sense of failure? Is it just too private? Does it allude to undisclosed medical conditions? I am though, going to try this as a topic of conversation soon with a fellow childless male friend, though I will need to pick my moment carefully.

There are, however, children in my life: my partner has a grown-up child, I am an uncle and my friends have children and I try hard to remember their birthdays. To these young people, although I am sure I offer something in the way of another adult, a way of being that some men grow-up to be, there is no role for me in terms of the day to day stuff of disciplining, helping with homework or buying school trousers.

The female friend who challenged me on my desire to have children has also confided that she knows women who have 'lowered that bar' in terms of partner material as their sense of child bearing urgency has increased. I wonder if those men are aware of this and how they feel? As it ever been any different? Is the couple bond really made by what you go through together as much as what you started out with? I'm now at the age when some of my friends with children have painful separations under their belt and negotiations of weekend access to sort out. Maybe this is what I am scared of.

Given these circumstances, I'll need to rely on the others to explore their experience of actually being fathers, of how they have built upon and adapted what they saw in their households when growing up and whether, it is indeed the core of their masculinity. I'd also be interested in the issues I see other parents dealing with, of aligning professional identities with the need to leave early when a child is sick. Do they feel the pressure to 'be it all' that women feel? Who are the current role models for fatherhood and how does the reality match up?

Best,

Pete

Dear Pete, John and Sandy,

I'm struck on reading everyone's autobiographical account of 'work' that it's quite similar to my own. I grew up with both parents working, or rather I did for most of my childhood and teenage years; I still remember when my mum went 'back to work' when I was, I think, in Primary 2 or 3 at school, because it was a significant break with family routine. She ended up working as a cleaner in a hospital (I remember my dad and us dropping her off at the Edinburgh Royal Infirmary one Christmas Day, not a good shift) and, later, in various secretarial positions, always part-time and relatively poorly paid.

My dad worked throughout, at first with British Telecom, or rather the old General Post Office before BT was split off prior to privatisation; some of his work tools even years later were emblazoned with either 'GPO' or 'El Torro', his nickname among colleagues. I remember feeling quite proud that my dad had a nickname, which (in my childhood mind) denoted popularity among his peers. My dad worked a lot, and he was often away on 'courses', usually in the Scottish Borders, although I never really understood what he did on these courses beyond drinking too much (not, I hasten to add, in a bad way). In fact, he was probably a workaholic, a tendency I recognise in myself as I get older. But I'm pretty sure he enjoyed his work, which to me is incredibly important, although of course he had all the usual frustrations about lack of promotion, poor pay and so on. Those were mostly removed in my teens, when my dad moved into the private sector doing the same job but not for BT Despite being ardently anti-Thatcher (and an SNP activist), privatisation and later deregulation of the telecoms sector did my dad a lot of good, not just in terms of earnings, but in job opportunities, an irony he acknowledged himself a lot later on.

So, I grew up in a household where both my parents worked and thus was raised with the expectation that work was a normal part of (grown-up) life. In retrospect I realise this wouldn't have been the case with a lot of my contemporaries. My parents' respective occupations also, in retrospect, fitted into standard gender-specific roles (and, I suppose, working class ones) in that my dad had a manual/technical job and my mum, like many women then and now, part-time work in administration or cleaning. I was conscious of this more when I met my dad's colleagues on days off school and so on when my brother and I might end up going to an old telephone exchange (fascinating places) or, later, workshops in Granton. A lot of them were gruff, working-class Irishmen, and my dad fitted right in.

When I went off to university in 1995, the point at which I began to move out of my class and certain childhood expectations, my (twin) brother worked with my dad for a year, so I saw even more of what my dad did during that period because my brother did too. In fact my dad was a bit cynical about me or indeed either of us going to uni because he couldn't really see the point, and had a rather old-fashioned notion that we might end up working for him, which would have been a respectable enough career but hardly an intellectually satisfying one. My mum generally thought the opposite that we should both get degrees, but both my parents were very hands off in that respect and didn't really push us one way or the other.

Quite a bit later on I remember my mum's reaction when I was unemployed for about six months in early 2007; I can only describe this as shame. In fact she was appalled and I remember being quite upset when she instructed me not to mention it to my uncle (her brother) at a Christmas family gathering. I'm quite sure he wouldn't have given a shit but she was betraying, I think, a certain working-class stigma about unemployment, something I imagine doesn't exist to the same extent these days. She quickly relaxed when I got work again, although she never quite adjusted to me being freelance, mainly because she couldn't understand how that worked in financial terms and, given the nature of my work (journalism), I ended up going through good and bad phases in terms of earning. Given her generation, my mum just couldn't understand how anyone could have such an unstable existence.

In stark contrast to my rather idle school and university days, I realise in retrospect that both my parents indirectly instilled in me what might be called the Presbyterian work ethic, which I think was a good thing. They remain slightly baffled by what I do – even though they can often see and read my output – but I suspect they're happy that I am actually working, as is my brother in a similar milieu. To this day I'm acutely conscious – always – of what the average UK income is and I measure my activity and earnings accordingly. If I earn about £25k a year I feel I'm doing okay, if I earn below, I feel anxious. In general terms I'm earning more than both my parents ever did (although it fluctuates), which feels a bit weird.

Cheers,

David

CHAPTER THREE

Is there a Crisis of Men and Scottish Men?

Is masculinity in crisis? Diane Abbott MP has been vocal recently about an issue close to our discussions. She calls it a 'crisis' of masculinity. For me, this raises two questions. Firstly, is she right? And secondly, regardless of the answer to the first, what is our role in helping with issues around gender and the dark-side of masculinity in general?

From our writing so far, I would say that whilst there have been changes in how masculinity is expressed, we have found advantage in the changes brought by feminism. Is the crisis of masculinity really a crisis that belongs to younger men? Is it more of a crisis for those who haven't found a place for themselves in society through paid work or belonging to a tribe from which they can take self-esteem and pride? Identity through work is becoming increasing precarious, not offering the kind of community recognition that working in older industries did. We all seem to have done OK by it though. The new gender landscape offers us possibility and opportunity – which we have taken.

Perhaps we are in danger of sounding smug. But *if* there is a crisis of masculinity are we somehow complicit in it? We may not be the absent fathers, abusers or perpetrators of violence that offer little in the way of positive role models for younger men but are men in society generally absent in other ways? Absent in the debates about pornography, abuse and violence? Is it enough to dissociate ourselves from it – to plead 'Not me, guv' innocence whilst sticking to 'bigger' topics such as the future of the Scottish Nation, party politics or the global economy?

I know others in this conversation are professionally involved in dealing with the consequences and causes of the dark side of masculinity. But away from our work roles – are we part of the problem?

Pete

31 MAY 2013

I'm not sure we can say it's a 'crisis' in masculinity, this seems to presume that we all have a common and clear understanding of what masculinity is and means, I'm not sure we do, I don't. I think in my lifetime the things men do and are expected to do has changed. This is inextricably linked to what has happened to women and sometimes as a direct consequence. Although it does occur to me that I'm really not sure what the male equivalent is to 'feminism'. I think feminism is viewed mostly as a positive movement, ethos, or 'thing'. It is also my impression that feminism has been a fight and the 'enemy' has been men. In defining what women want in terms of equality the narrative is usually, certainly often, that men acting in concert like some generic homogenous group are the barriers to feminism winning the fight. It is as if all men are responsible for the sexism that exists and occurs everywhere, is perpetuated in media, magazines and internet and that is our fault as well.

Much of this media stuff defines women but men too are subject to this type of this everyday sexism but when we use the word sexism we presume it's about women. Much of the drive for gender equality has been driven by feminism and is viewed through that single prism. I think many of us men have recognised that women have a good case, we feel a bit guilty about it all, we recognise the unfairness of things and support their cause and accept their language about men accepting that they don't mean us but other men; we are not afforded the same leeway in language. Have we allowed this argument debate to be too one-sided? Has our guilt about the unfairness meant we have just allowed it to happen and not really paid attention to what is really happening? I'm sure men die younger than women in every or most societies in the world. What does that say?

Maybe young men today behave the way they do because of their frustration, I think they do, their alienation. We understand the journey feminism has been on and where it is now, younger men maybe just see women everywhere doing all jobs, jobs that they will now view as 'women's' jobs. No men in nurseries, few men in teaching and decreasing all the time in police, social services, everywhere. Single person households in the UK are 29 per cent, in Glasgow it's 43 per cent. Is it a West of Scotland thing? Are we needed?

Could our crisis be more about feminism? Could the crisis be real but we are missing the real point? Has our guilt made us accede to every issue raised by women as requiring change without actually thinking about the consequences or the real meaning?

John

1 JUNE 2013

Men's lower life expectancy in global terms may be a red herring – a biological inequality rather than a social one. What I think is significant is the fact men are more likely to die of suicide – three times more likely than women in Scotland [1]. I think this points to crucial differences in how men respond, adapt and cope with stress. It may also point to differences in the availability of social support for men. That when men do face crisis and challenge, asking for help and support, having people to talk to, just doesn't feel an option. I don't think men's higher likelihood of choosing suicide reflects a difference in the severity of stress and challenge men face in society, but perhaps what it does reflect is that the challenges men face are not high enough on the agenda of current social concern, perhaps not even known. Take unemployment. Yes, this is high priority concern for politicians and society but is addressed as a macro economic problem rather than in the personal, emotional or existential terms that would lead us to understanding its mental health consequences. Is this a consequence of women campaigning for and winning equality? No, I don't think so. It is about how men relate to other men and how politics operates. To take the brand of politics I grew up with – varieties of socialism, I am struck about how little room for the personal there was within it.

To take John's points about feminism, I think the concept can be caricatured to be about the problem with men. Of course, it was never meant to be about men per se but about the system of power and control that arose from having men in charge for centuries. This made certain inequalities in society feel natural and inevitable (and I'm sorry for this caricature!). The very fact we can have the conversation we are having, about the possibilities of new masculinities, shows how far feminist thinking has permeated our consciousness – that we consider 'maleness' as not a fixed certainty like a point on the compass but open for constant negotiation and change.

But are we comfortable with any of this? Are men confortable with talking in a manner that isn't about either finding solutions ('let's fix this') or negotiating superiority ('my opinion has more credibility than yours') – two directions I often find conversations with men going. In an age where the skills that male labour used to provide can now be done by machines – or done in developing countries for a fraction of the cost- it is the emotional, relational and supportive aspects of labour that is in demand; the counsellors, teachers, mentors, customer service and sales reps, hairdressers and other varieties of therapist. As these are roles utilising 'feminine' skills, then perhaps this explains why some see a society as a pitched battle between genders in which women have the ascendancy (you only need to look at comparative rates of pay and hours in unpaid domestic labour to see that they are not).

Pete

3 JUNE 2013

To be absolutely honest, I haven't thought in any depth about masculinity, which is until I responded to a *Scotsman* article by Gerry Hassan (and his BBC Scotland radio series) around two years ago. And, of course, when he invited me to get involved with this discussion. I guess I don't really think in those terms, and – unlike some of you – I don't have any professional need to think in those terms. I'm also guilty of not being very self-analytical in that respect (although I am in others), I suppose because I consider myself almost above the fray to some extent (being gay). Gerry mentioned my twitter retort (which got me into trouble with some feminists – as well as Gerry!) that I considered myself 'metrosexual', i.e. I didn't like being categorised as 'a man'. I tweeted this in jest, but at the same time I was only half joking.

To me it's a slightly old-fashioned debate, and I guess that's my perspective as the youngest in our group (forgive me if this sounds at all patronising). I grew up in the 1990s (I was only 12 when the 1980s drew to a close, and I wasn't a very politically-aware pre-teen), and my political consciousness only kicked in post-1997 and – to be honest –

debates about masculinity, gender and so on didn't feature during my period of student activism or, indeed, beyond (but then I was involved with the Scottish Tories, so that isn't altogether surprising). And if I'm being honest, I'm still not convinced it's a problem. Is there a crisis in male masculinity? Not really. But then if I'm being even more honest, this is the viewpoint of a reasonably comfortably off white male freelance journalist who's comfortable with his own sexuality and generally enjoying life. I'm lucky in that respect, so I wouldn't pretend to be truly representative, even of my own peer group.

So, thinking about it a little more yes, there are certainly issues around (Scottish/male) masculinity, but I'm not sure any of it amounts to what could be termed a 'crisis'. I'm not a fan of exaggerating phenomena – a very politician-like thing to do. We touched upon several of these issues when we met in Glasgow, and again I feel a little aloof from most of them. To an extent, I might even have subconsciously jettisoned most traditional forms of masculinity as a child, ie my father's sincere efforts to get me to like football and golf, both of which failed profoundly. Obviously the pursuit of girls was out (although I suppose in gay parlance I am, or so I'd like to think, 'masculine', but that came much later), as was binge drinking on beer (which I didn't start imbibing until a few years ago), and so on and so forth.

My disengagement from all this does not mean, of course, that problems don't exist, it's just that I struggle to explore them in any depth. That might change in the course of these exchanges!

David

8 JUNE 2013

David's last piece highlights that if there is a crisis around masculinity, it is not men *per se* who are in crisis – we have all, to varying degrees, shown our comfort in the current gender landscape in these exchanges. In fact, I do not personally know any men who appear in crisis about their gender identities. At least, not in a profound way. Maybe in a fleeting, slightly knowing and arch, 'Am I real man?' type way. Traditional masculinity is to my peers is something to engage in playfully – I'm resisting saying ironically.

I'll give you an example. I'm writing this on a train on my way to meet some friends I grew up with. We are celebrating the 40th birthday of one of them. Out of the four of us, it is the birthday boy who most outwardly appears to embrace a traditional masculine identity. In fact, in recognition of this layer of his being, we have bought him a tankard and had it engraved. Everyone is in agreement this is the perfect present for this guy. The gift of a tankard alludes to the lives of men in a by-gone age, when you would put yours behind the bar of your local along with the drinking vessels of the other men. The tankard as an idea is heavy in emotion and symbolism. It is a gift possibly given to you by another man (your father?), referring to an activity engaged elbow-to-elbow with other men showing you are accepted in their company. My father once tried to buy me a tankard for my 21st birthday but I found out and put a stop to it. The idea of the tankard made me cringe with embarrassment. I didn't want to be in that particular club. Perhaps I felt the symbolism inappropriate coming from my father. The young narcissist in me also pained from my father simply 'not getting' what I was about.

There are so many layers here I'm not sure where to start. Let's start with my friend. Actually, this guy is not that bothered by his masculine identity. What does animate him is social class. Proudly working class by background (mother a cleaner, father unable to work) he is now firmly ensconced in commuter belt gentility. He plays golf, sends his son to rugby. At University he won prizes and a First class degree and achieved it all with hard work, ingenuity and (let's not forget this) state support. The tankard for him (and us) represents a knowing nod to the lives we came from with its assumptions of what kind of life you had laid out before you (as I have alluded to earlier, this way of living was actually being systematically dismantled). The tankard, if you over think it, may allude to the certainty of peoples' assumptions that made of other ways of being (the ones we had) 'weird', a bit fruity with the suspicion of homosexuality constantly hanging over you – suspicions we gleefully accepted. Actually being gay would have been cooler than our humdrum heterosexuality with its attendant risks of inelegance, boorishness and parochialism. I now realise being gay doesn't preclude these but forgive us our adolescent presumptions.

A point here is that for many men, masculinity is 'post gay'. I find David's point that being gay puts him 'above the fray' fascinating. Is being a gay man not a form of masculinity in and of itself? Further, is it not a form of masculine identity that can claim most credit (perhaps alongside David Beckham) for re-defining the parameters of contemporary masculinity in recent decades?

Perhaps this is why David thinks the debate sounds old fashioned. I agree the crisis in masculinity is an over simplification for 'why young urban men are failing?' Perhaps our politicians and media have difficulty in talking in terms of more than one concept; ethnicity, class, sexuality or gender – always 'or' never 'and'. But David offers us some clear markers of what Scottish masculine identity might be – specifically 'football, golf, chasing girls and beer'. Given the profound changes in gender roles in Scottish society, why does this list look so dated? What else would be on this list?

Pete

10 JUNE 2013

I've just spent the last 48 hours trying to readjust to normal life after eight days cycling and camping in Mull with three other guys. Old mates going back 20 years plus. More of this later.

So, I'm coming into the debate now. I like it. There is just so much I want to reply to. Pete's tankard story is a beaut, but I won't pick up on this one for the moment.

Having read all the recent contributions in a oner I am driven by the urge to coin a kind of summary. All three of you question whether there is actually a crisis at all with masculinity, but from different positions. David wants some evidence that it deserves the label 'crisis'. Pete speculates on whether it is really only a crisis for young men. David's 'above the fray' comment may even hint at the supposed masculinity crisis being a more specifically heterosexual crisis. Pete has a go at some definition of 'masculine qualities' – fixing things and taking charge.

Pete simultaneously introduces 'the darker side of men'. John picks up on this theme by questioning whether we men accept the blame too much. Pete and David in their different ways speak of the clear pluses that have come out this 'sexual revolution' for them and most of their male friends. John doesn't deny this this but speaks of 60 years of dramatic change in the social and domestic landscape that sound to me as much of a journey for John himself as for most of the people he knew –men and women (apologies John if I'm putting words into your mouth).

For me John comes closest to acknowledging the existence of a crisis. A real problem that is not getting solved and shows all the signs of getting worse. A problem that is specifically and overwhelmingly experienced and committed by males. John understandably refers to crime and social stats. I could match those stats with employment stats and the steady year on year shift toward female dominance in growing high paid professions and showing all the signs of exponential rise. Sorry Pete, but I thought your use of female domestic wages missed the point. Domestic work; cleaning of any kind, whether by women or men, is always going to command the bottom wages. Men already are and will increasingly be the cleaners of the future and the wages won't go magically up.

There is a problem and it's key characteristic is that the subjects are male. The stats on violence of all sorts, crime generally, literacy, numeracy, general exam passes, graduations, suicides, road accidents, child care orders, health in old age, substance and sexual addictions (yes, the massive porn industry) – are ALL overwhelmingly negative for males specifically. Men are in trouble. And because we are a society of both men and women, we are all in trouble.

Certainly the term 'crisis in masculinity' struck a chord as I shared our project with the guys I spent last week with – on the white sandy beaches of Mull over the odd malt whisky and bonfire. Take the 45-year-old father who works in the finance sector in Edinburgh. A strong SNP activist from a very working class agriculture background in West Lothian. He has a girl at secondary and a boy at primary. His main and indeed immediate contribution to the debate was that he didn't think it was good for the boys in his son's primary school for there not to be a single man anywhere in the building. He just thought it can't be right, on so many levels, for boys to never see a man during the school day.

But finally I want to focus on one point from the above gruesome list – suicide. It sounds to me you are saying Pete that men commit suicide more because they don't have the emotional intelligence or skills to cope with stuff of life as women do. It reminds me of a song from *My Fair Lady* – but in reverse – 'Why can't a man be more like a woman?' This has always been the hint at the heart of feminism that I find disturbing. I fear that if we only see the dark in one half of our collective human species then we will drive the darkness in the other half (women) underground only to emerge as sadism.

For me the story of human history is one of both genders. As Hobbes said of the past: 'solitary, poor, nasty, brutish and short'. He didn't say 'only for women.' Are we really saying that at no time did any women have a better time of it than any men? Yes, John. Men have taken too much of the blame. Where we are now is a dynamic between the genders. Stuff needed to change, and change it has. Many of us – as Pete and David so rightly point out, has been to the benefit of men – some men. But millions of our gender are being left behind, are suffering and dying disproportionally – and that is a crisis.

And really finally – the case for action should be clear but what is missing is a shared politics and ideology on how to tackle the problem. In reading the exchanges one line jumped out more than any other. It was when John asked whether it isn't really a crisis in feminism. In other words (my words) a crisis in the socially and governmentally dominant feminist strategies for addressing gender inequality and injustice. They don't work.

Well, you wanted controversy.

Sandy

14 JUNE 2013

Sandy, your point that we are all in this together is important. Is this perception of a 'crisis' just that, a perception, ours, viewed from our personal stand point, our age, our experience? Maybe because Sandy and I are of a similar age (sorry, assuming) we have witnessed and experienced more of the shift in roles. I don't mean that we know better because we do not, but we have experienced more of the change first hand and it is not imperceptible.

I find the mention of suicide particularly relevant. I attended a funeral yesterday of a 21-year-old man, the son of a colleague. He was a piper and played at my daughter's wedding. He took his own life last week. There were 1,000 people at his funeral, yet on Saturday night after being out with his friends he killed himself. He lived with his mum and dad, and younger sister. He was joining the police.

It may be a little late in our conversations to quote some figures to illustrate the 'crisis' but:

- 90% of school children with behavioural problems are boys
- 80% of pupils with learning difficulties are boys
- 81% of pupil exclusions are boys
- 90% of court appearances are males between 16–24
- 90% of all violent crime is committed by men
- 84% of suicide victims are men aged 16–24.

I spoke with a teacher this week, she teaches Modern Studies in Lanarkshire, she has a higher stream at the moment with 28 pupils of whom only five are boys.

The success of girls in education compared to boys may partly be as a result of having positive female role models in their life, at home and in school. There are few positive male role models for boys, the stats I quoted last time about single person households confirm the trend. These stats also point to fewer successful relationships and when these do break down, in the vast majority of cases, it's the males who absent themselves from the family leaving women to bring up children. Maybe young boys do not see any role for themselves even as 'fathers' in the broadest sense of that term. Men are physically and biologically capable of becoming fathers but their commitment to that role seems to stop there for many they have no experience of fatherhood or fathering. I agree with Sandy, Pete's story of the tankard is a beaut but for lots of young men there is no father to give a gift, even an inappropriate one. We had some gang members on an outward bound course with the army two years ago. During the week away one of the guys turned 18 and we bought him a cake, gave him a knife to cut it, he had never had a birthday cake in his life.

It's too easy to say that since suicide is self-directed violence and violence is a male thing it's not surprising more males commit suicide. The point is why do so many Scottish males choose this as a response to personal challenges in their life, professional, relationship etc?

From the invasion of Afghanistan in 2001 and Iraq in 2003 until October 2010 (7/10/2001 to 3/10/2010) **43** Scottish service men lost their lives in these conflicts. In the same period **5,624** men in Scotland committed suicide, you might need to read that a couple of times, I did. Where is the war being fought? Where are the men most at risk?

Scotland has one of the highest rates of suicide in Europe, if not the highest. Perhaps if we think of alienation and what that means in terms of disconnect, responsibility and involvement we may be close to focusing on the challenge of masculinity.

I'm not suggesting that we should roll back decades of change towards a more gender equal society, but there are often unforeseen or unexpected outcomes or consequences to such significant change and maybe what we are sensing as individuals are these outcomes. Our perceptions of the consequences will differ because we are all of us different in age, background and education and many other ways. We are perhaps making some assumptions about our life experiences and backgrounds and presuming they permit us some particular insight into the thoughts, challenges and ambitions of young men today? Not sure they do and I'm certain that we cannot put all young men into some homogenous group.

I suspect for well educated young men brought up by thoughtful parents not much will have changed in terms of life opportunities. They will have the capacity to deal with the challenges of life they encounter in the context of the world they experience and know that they are supported by their family friends and their collective positive life experiences.

Maybe this is why David is relaxed about the notion of masculinity. Perhaps Sandy and I are a little more alarmed because we have witnessed far more change. For many well educated young men the world is fine, it's what they expected, it's all they know and for them there is no significant change, so far, it's always been like this and why wouldn't it be? The world inhabited by the young man who didn't ever have a birthday is what he expected, it's what he knows.

Have a great day, stay away from the sun, and David, tie your laces!!

John

CHAPTER FOUR

Being a Man: Men, Women, Masculinity and Femininity

24 JUNE 2013

Dear David, John and Sandy,

The last two pieces from Sandy and John have been by far the most powerful in these exchanges. The statistics John provides are in no way surprising but still have the power to stop you in your tracks. However familiar these statistics, they are a cause for societal-wide shame. I suspect men have always out-stripped women across the problems he identifies, and this is not to down-play them. Partly as a consequence of the processes by which you become recorded as one of these statistics (a school exclusion, a criminal, a suicide) but partly because the traits which lead to them have always fitted better within the realms of socially acceptable behaviours for men than for women. I go back to one of John's earlier posts recalling his childhood and the then commonly and oft recounted memories of the Second World War: fighting as a positive masculine trait, when used as a power for good; for protection or for a greater more worthy aim. I am not saying that violence and aggression are necessarily male characteristics, it's just that we have had greater support for such responses provided in the role models we have presented to us. If not violence *per se*, being able to dominate and exploit your environment, to shape it to your will. Unlike the collective endeavour of the Second World War however, this often is presented to us, as through being a strong, determined individual, doing it alone.

This is how I would respond to Sandy's interpretation of my view in his last post: 'that men commit suicide more because they don't have the emotional intelligence or skills to cope with stuff of life as women do'. To be clear, I would resist assigning any trait as being innately connected to the biological characteristics between the sexes. I might argue however that for men historically, emotional intelligence has not been a quality on which they have been appraised. One potential proof of this is in the fact that the very phrase 'emotional intelligence' only came into currency after the feminist revolution. Some women do not have much of it either and many men do. We learn empathy and emotional intelligence as much as we are born with it. Where do we learn it? The usual places, the home, the school, the workplace, through society's expectations of us. One of the absences flowing from the growing exclusion of men from families, primary schools, nurseries and the workplace lies in that lost opportunity for boys and young men to learn such skills through interactions with other men, through mentored trial and error, and learning what underpins positive relationships in the longer term.

Further, perhaps women respond to despair in different ways than men, choosing other self-destructive behaviours which are not recorded as suicide but have at their heart the same sense of existential void. In my own family, I can think of two women dear to me for whom I suspect this was the case. If a woman chooses to fill the void with alcohol night after night, year after year, it becomes a liver cirrhosis statistic, not suicide. Of course, this is not an option confined to women. Another explanation is that women have culturally been allowed to have support networks and coping strategies that enable different responses. As Sandy told us in an earlier post, a school counsellor was kept busier by female students. This was not because girls had more problems to be solved than boys. Clearly, however, seeking the counsellor's help was more consistent with the idea of being a girl than a boy.

So, am I saying 'if only men were more like women'? I am not. Masculinity and femininity are not fixed entities. Their enactment changes over time, across and within cultures. What shapes them is often not the choice of individuals but the needs of that society and economy. Ours needs fewer warriors now in the same way it needs less coal miners or ship builders. Yet, for decades, it did and we shaped ourselves and each other to be able to fill these roles (not just men, our mothers, lovers and teachers shaped us also). The needs of that time are not as easily wiped from the cultural landscape as the chimney stacks and pit gear is from the physical.

Feminism was never a zero-sum game with one side winning and the other losing. We were all meant to win. Remember, the feminist perspective holds that if it was women who were in charge of our financial institutions then we would not have had the crash of 2007. That claim is hard to prove but it is credible to suggest the financial melt-down was caused by the actions of men acting in traditionally alpha male ways. The economic conditions which shape the hopelessness of many young men's lives, denying them roles and sources of esteem, is much more about the inequalities between the financial *haves* and *have nots* than between the genders. It's a story of one group squeezing out every last pound of profit through efficiencies that outside of our financial centres translates into no work or work that is hard to use as a secure foundation of self-esteem and identity. Employing women over men often is one of these efficiencies, not because they have more power, but because they will do the same job for less than men. If men being more like women means getting paid less, then no, I do not think this is the way forward.

John's mention of alienation jumps out at me as the most credible explanation of the predicament of contemporary men. Not in itself a result of the gains of feminism. A new enactment of masculinity does indeed need to be negotiated and discovered. This is in response not only the challenge thrown down by feminism to traditionally male ways of being but also changing technology and the nature of work. For this task, more fertile ground is found when there is work to be done and land over the horizon to head for. Many men are not finding themselves in the roles we find ourselves – leading public or professional lives with a common sense of purpose, a cause to which you can contribute and a role to define and play. This shapes private lives as well as public and the exclusion of men from child-rearing is as much down to their financial exclusion as any other form.

Pete

Hi guys,

Not sure of this is out of turn but I'm still doing a lot of travelling so I need to make use of the time I have to respond. As always, I hope it makes some sense. I think the notion of alienation deserves more time but this response is really around violence, not specifically domestic violence, Nigella Lawson and her violent husband for example, but more general.

Pete's observation that violence and aggression are not necessarily exclusively or inherently male traits is interesting. I agree but I do think these traits are expected to be of more use to men than women. Perhaps mothers, believing that strong males/sons able to look after/protect themselves and their families is a necessary and an attractive male trait encourage 'strong' behaviour in their sons. Maybe we have as a society evolved dramatically changing roles and behaviours, but perhaps the biological evolution takes longer and we're not quite there with that yet.

I'm not sure of the science but the notion of how we behave and interact with our environment and other people must have something to do with learned experience as well as our inherent human biology/physiology/psychology (told you I'm no good at the science!). Richard Tremblay is a Professor of child psychiatry at Ottawa University who has carried out work on aggression in children, two longitudinal studies, I think. He was in Scotland a few years ago and I met him. When I asked him how we learn to be violent, he suggested that my question was the wrong way round and that we in fact learn *not* to be violent.

When we think about Tremblay's suggestion in the context of what we know about the importance of the early years it does make sense. The first three years of life is the time when we learn empathy and acquire a suite non-cognitive skills that allow us to communicate, negotiate, compromise; skills which then allow us to judge risk, make good decisions about ourselves and deal with life's challenges. If we learn other options, violence then becomes a last resort, available if required in life threatening situations, but not used summarily to deal with all situations. Now think about the gender imbalance relating to levels of suicide, which is self-directed violence.

These early years skills are acquired from those adults around us and they will be influenced to conform to what they experience or believe is the norm. So a young man born into a violent household and living in an area where interpersonal violence is present in other situations, will learn to adapt to that environment, it's what humans do – we adapt. I think this touches on several of Pete's observations, the influence of our caregivers, and the needs of our society.

I think too this propensity for violence would have been tempered and bounded by conformities learned from interaction with other men, fathers, brothers, peers, work mates. I suppose I am saying that the absence of many of these governing influences is having a cumulative impact on young men. The opportunities to acquire these governing skills are being reduced, single parents, broken relationships, absent fathers, fewer extended families, fewer male teachers, less male dominated work environments. In fact there will be times when the male presence can be a significant negative influence and reinforce aggression and violence as legitimate responses.

I'm sure that mothers instinctively prepare their sons for the life they believe they will live – a life often perceived by them to be about aggression and violence where there will at some point be a need to fight for something. The old story about the young Scots boy who gets beaten up by a big boy at school and runs crying to his mum and she tells him to get back out and fight his own battles. She will encourage in him an absolute and non-negotiable need to stand up for himself and not to back down to anyone in any circumstance, I suggest that this is mistakenly referred to as 'respect' and many young men are obsessed by it, not just in Scotland.

It may be that while women are evolving to embrace a new world of equality and opportunity (comparatively) men are not. Perhaps since feminism is driving the change, there is clear ownership in this new order. It's what is wanted and needed. There is an almost universal presumption that the change is for good, it's deserved and should be embraced and celebrated. As a consequence men are forced to be more responsive and are reacting to the changes. For them the changes are not seen as negotiated and are therefore sometimes resented.

John

18 JUNE 2013

Hi all,

Firstly my apologies for the delay. I had a whole piece nearly written but a bug wiped it out last weekend. So, back to where I was. I feel moved to make a statement on where I'm coming from afresh, rather than pick up on the debate (interesting as it has been) so far. So, here goes… again…

My key point is balance and history. By that I mean, what I hope for is a way forward with the topic of masculinity that is balanced. One that does not see the dynamic between the genders in terms of goodies and baddies. And one that sees the future in terms of trying to support a healthier relationship between the genders for the sake of the species. For this reason I have revised my position. I don't see this 'problem' as a problem with men per se. If there is a perceived problem with one gender then there is by default a problem with both genders. Humanity has male and female and for the future sake of our species we need to find a way of getting along better.

Which brings me to history. The revolution in gender relations is but half a century old. The immense changes in the west have happened in less than a single lifespan. From total domination by men in virtually all professions, trades and positions of power we now live in a society where it is questionable whether males of any age in the future can be sure of being served by any male teachers or doctors at all. Already, as we have discussed, primary schools are overwhelmingly dominated by women and now approaching 60 per cent of GPs are women. These are trends that show no sign of reversing. The Boys' Club ghettos are falling like nine pins. In the financial and equity worlds, which I have recently encountered through my charity, these sectors too are increasingly dominated at the younger end by infinitely smarter young women. And yet we have to contend with the same old rather tired complaining about those very few times (and therefore newsworthy) when some television debate has a predominately or sometimes, all male panel. (Something I experience at virtually every meeting I go to – being the only man present and the women in the main don't notice it or even think it matters.)

Slavery ended nearly 200 years ago, yet it took that long to achieve a black president of a major power. Let us take a longer perspective and see the trends. Remember that we are not seeking (or at least I hope not) a world where the patriarchal domination of the past is simply reversed into a matriarchal domination. Because unless we do something, that is what is going to happen certainly in the west. Disenfranchised, devalued, disrespected women of the past will be replaced by the mirror image. But because men were once so totally in charge, they feel the pain and loss often acutely and behaviour can become ugly.

My take on the debate so far is that John and I see this, but David and Pete less so. I think this is because (as John mentioned) he and I have lived through these changes and remember a world when being a typical man was unrecognisable from what we see today. I think that both David and Pete have experienced more of the plus side of the gender revolution in their adult lives and see little in the way of a 'problem' at work or at home. For me this just shows the sheer pace of change. Pete (I guess) is but 15 years younger than me. Nothing in historical terms. But his life passage seems not to have exposed him to the lost-ness of men as men. David on the other hand made a very interesting point. Maybe this is after all a problem with heterosexual men. And maybe it is. But we can't create (nor would we wish) a world where being heterosexual is seen as something to be cured and replaced by homosexuality. Say goodbye to the human race – unless it's all going to be test tubes from now on.

We are a predominately heterosexual species made up of potentially breeding males and females. It is true that the middle classes appear to be faring better. Jobs in those sectors are mixed and employment policies and anti-discriminating regulations mean that we learn how to behave better to each other – and keep any other thoughts to ourselves. The misogyny goes underground.

And this is the thing that bothers me most about the whole gender equality debate. Men and women are equal – right? They have always been equal – even in the eyes of God (if you're a believer of some sort). So any variance of that is in some ways 'wrong'. In my view, over a debatable number of millennia, we created a politics across western and Middle Eastern societies where men were seen as superior (to varying degrees) spiritually, morally, intellectually and evolutionarily, to women. That's how it's been. I don't dispute it. Now the feminists and their fellow travellers can crow and push for just one more hollow regulatory victory. Or they can act like stateswomen and think about the road ahead.

Power never was wholly in the hands of men. If we were created equal then as equal humans we will be active. Women have been very powerful in the spheres of life where they were able to be. Who was not hugely influenced by their mothers or other women in their families? As I've said before – if one is bad then the other has no vent to their sadism.

It's a 'wake up and smell the coffee' moment. The stats are overwhelming. The pendulum is swinging so fast the other way – it's unstoppable. There WILL be a world (certainly in the west dominated economies) where mainly women will be in charge of the decisions affecting most people's lives. No use complaining, disputing or celebrating: it's the maths. Short of a worldwide plague affecting only under 30–year-olds or a brain virus affect new born females, we will be led primarily by women in another 50 years. And that's assuming the same pace of change as the last 50 years.

So, how do we address the re-negotiation of the male/female relationship? That is the question facing us. Can women be less vengeful, cruel and hateful then men were? I hope so, for our children's sake – both girls as well as boys. Boys and men think differently to girls and women. It's not just misogynistic conditioning. In the main our brains are wired differently. It's not about outdoing the other gender on every totem of power. It's about finding out, understanding and being genuinely curious about how each gender works and thrives in a future where neither is so blatantly cruel to the other.

I could go on, and maybe I will at some point. But that's all for now.

Sandy

24 JUNE 2013

Apologies if this response is out of sync, again, I'm in Italy and the internet access is like lots of other things here, intermittent and unreliable!! Otherwise Argegno on Lake Como is fab. Also why I've been quiet, sorry.

I'm not sure we have adequately defined what we consider to be the problem. We have all mentioned masculinity but is it just a problem of the male role in society? If it is role, then what role? Is it a relationship role: father, brother, son, husband? Is it a working role: job, career, leader, provider?

It seems to me that we are wrong to think of this as one-dimensional; it's too easy to frame it as a threat from feminism and the changing role of women. I think too that feminism seems to be a little narrow and we have discussed this briefly in previous exchanges.

Are these 'isms' not at heart about equality and if they are then do we really think we have this notion of equality sussed, what it really means.

We are, as humans, evolutionary animals and I'm not sure we can all be equal and I'm not sure that would be a good thing anyway. Some of us are taller, some are smarter, some are faster, and some are stronger and so on. There are differences and it's our human characteristics that have recognised these differences and formed partnerships and collaboration to work more effectively together to achieve agreed goals. When our ingenuity and knowledge increased we invented machines to help us fill the gaps in our abilities, computers think faster but sadly bombs also kill more effectively.

Males and females are different, biologically, psychologically and physically, and I suspect it's very difficult if not impossible to change this, it's how we have evolved and these differences create a mutual dependency. Perhaps in a few millennium there will be a new gender that is wholly self-sufficient.

I think it's in these differences that the real challenge lies. The debate around women being the equal of men misses the point completely, that's not equal that's just measurement against what is perceived to be the current dominant force within a value system created by men for men. The roles that are best undertaken by men are valued above those best undertaken by women and it's been like this for a long time, it's easy to understand why 'equality' has become so focused on gender equality.

In the current commercialisation of the world, money has become the only measure of value or success and with it comes power and influence. It's not surprising then that women have come to believe that they must do what men do to get valued and have striven to get into jobs that pay well and have power. But how many women in the boardroom, how many on TV, how many CEOs, how many chief constables, how many MPs is not really a measure of gender equality.

I'm suggesting that our challenge is not to engage in the argument that women are better than men, or men better than women, but to create a real debate around equality so that whatever we are doing is valued. This will require a new way to set value beyond money.

In relation to perceived roles for men and women it all seems to be one way at the moment. Women need and deserve equality, but by doing everything men can do as well as being a mother has consequences for that relationship. To be clear I am saying that we need more gender equality but we need to also understand better the outcomes for families, relationships and individuals as we move to more equality particularly if that equality is only about work. We need also to better value traditional female roles, or perhaps the genie is out of the bottle.

Sandy's point about all male panels on TV programmes is well made. When I speak to early years' workers or health visitors the audiences, without exception, will be all female. If it's about teachers, it's about 75 per cent of women, that's not equality.

If women can lead, men can nurture, I suppose this is true but can we do it equally well? I expect some men can but I'm not sure all men can. We need to value the role of looking after children more than we do. Do we think if nursery workers were paid on the same scale as university lecturers we would get more men doing it? If men were not portrayed as often as predatory paedophiles posing an undefined threat to all children in all circumstances would more men be primary school teachers or scout leaders?

Back to the sun and coffee and the wine,

John

24 JUNE 2013

Dear chaps,

First of all, apologies for my long silence: I had a book to finish, but now this is being edited I have a little more time to spare for what is still an interesting discussion.

I'm very struck by what Sandy says about Pete and I having experienced more of the 'plus side' of the gender revolution in our adult lives and thus perceive less of a 'problem' with male masculinity. I think broadly speaking that's true, although I'd be uncomfortable with the implication that for me it was all plan sailing. I didn't come out until my mid 20s (and had few sexual experiences until then), which even in the context of the late '90s/early '00s made me a 'late starter'. Sure, that changed rapidly – probably from the moment Scotland had a very public and often rancorous debate over the abolition of Section 28 in the year 2000 – and certainly there's evidence that suggests schools are now much more relaxed places where kids come to terms with their sexuality very early on. I can assure you that wasn't the case at Leith Academy in 1989 to 1995, nor even at Aberdeen University in 1995 to 1999. It's true that I'm now very relaxed about the whole thing, but given I'm approaching my 36th birthday that's a relatively recent thing, encompassing only the last decade or so. Even then, I was probably 30 before I was 'fully developed' in gay lifestyle terms. Sorry, these terms all sound very clunky on reading them back, but hopefully you'll know what I mean.

There is a class dimension to this, and I suspect this cuts across sexuality and gender. Middle class folk (in my experience) tend to be much more confident and dare I say it progressive in gender terms, ie relaxed about their own sexuality, confident in doing something about it, sensitivity and so on. Now obviously this is a generalisation, but it's always struck me as broadly true, and particularly *vis-à-vis* those lower down the pecking order. So I would posit that it isn't just, as Sandy suggested, 'a problem with heterosexual men', for I've met plenty of working-class gay men who are neither confident nor particularly happy.

Sandy also hinted at a general lessening of boundaries between homo and heterosexuality, male and female, and (again, broadly) I would agree with that. Even within the past ten years I have watched things relax considerably in those terms. The recent gay marriage debate is a good example of that. Would a male PM such as David Cameron felt as relaxed about extending the heterosexual preserve of marriage to gay men and women, say, ten years ago? I doubt it (indeed, he'd have voted against it). The evidence is also prevalent in the media, the 'metrosexual' David Beckham, etc. So it strikes me as a little odd to talk about a crisis of maleness when the evidence suggests that crisis ought to extend to women too. Isn't everything generally getting much more relaxed? I can't help feeling there'll be a huge shift, even between my generation and the next. Indeed, the students I know or meet are all even more relaxed about gender and sexuality than my immediate social circle.

Just some random thoughts. Looking forward to getting this going again.

Cheers,

David

29 JUNE 2013

Some more thoughts from the middle-aged jury!!

I think David's last contribution gets us closer to the issues we are all trying hard to describe. It maybe is an issue for both men and women each trying to cope with changing demands, expectations and boundaries within established and 'traditional' gender roles.

I know many women who are mothers and also work in paid employment and who will freely confess to feelings of guilt about not being at home with their children. I know not all women feel like this but I think there will be a sizeable number of working women who would much prefer to be at home with their children.

I'm not certain why these 'reluctant' working mums do it. It may be to earn more money to achieve a lifestyle that is imagined to be better, two cars, big house, etc. Maybe some do it because they think that it is expected of them because everyone else does it and the belief that everyone else is doing is a powerful motivation. There will of course be some working mums who do it because they can and they are taking advantage of their right to do it.

Whatever the reasons, the outcomes are the same and I think it is these outcomes that we are perhaps identifying from our own individual perspective and which we have initially identified as a crisis in masculinity. This is perhaps more true for Sandy and I since in our everyday jobs we encounter the failures and the feckless and our experience confirms commonality between many of those we have to deal with. I don't mean to imply that Pete and David don't have an appreciation of this challenge but rather it is more of a reality for Sandy and I because of our working experience and I expect, too, our age.

I don't think the issues around sexuality that both Sandy and David have spoken of provide the complete picture. Sexuality and the blurring of gender roles is not quite the same thing. It will be part of this general changing of roles for men and women and as David suggested this generation's attitude towards sexuality is very different from the last generation. But is there a direct connect between this relaxed attitude towards gender and sexuality and the outcomes we have identified as forming the 'crisis in masculinity?' I think I am quite relaxed about gender and sexuality but I am less relaxed about the changing roles of men and women and the negative impact this is having on children and families and relationships.

I agree with the class dimension as David suggested, and it makes the difference. The acceptance and understanding of these changing roles and I expect too sexuality is less impactive on middle class families than families in poorer circumstances. The negative outcomes are far more visible and immediate but a neglected child is the same, no matter where he/she lives and having your own room and a computer does not mean you are not a neglected child.

John

CHAPTER FIVE

Relationships and Professionals

Interesting how many of our email exchanges start with apologies for the time elapsed since our last contribution. Well, I won't break the tradition. I'm sorry for my silence over the last six weeks or so. I had a note for the first three, being on holiday (plans to keep my hand-in scuppered by poor antipodean wifi connections), jet lag for the fourth and an interview to prepare for in the fifth week. Now, back in the land of reliable broadband and body clock adjusted, my attentions can return to our masculinity project.

And with my usual sense of timing, it seemed I left just before the party got into full swing. I can't reply in a manner that does justice to the exchanges and stimulus material that had been fed in during my absence. But will try to order my thinking in response.

I was left thoughtful after Sandy's conversion to not seeing this as a problem of conflict between genders but a problem for both genders. This is what I have always seen feminism to be about. I love the idea of 'a social project to reinvent masculinity and gender roles in keeping with the world we have built' (Nelson article) but this has to involve women as well as men. Perhaps anticipating some of the discussion for the closing stages of this conversation, the absence of women in this discussion leaves a profound silence in the space between our musings.

A word recurring in my thoughts is 'alienation'. John raised it too. For me, I hear it in relation to how disconnected our society, led by the economy, has become to the, what Sandy describes as, 'the future sake of our species.' *If* the reason for biological sex differences is the continuation of our species, then culturally this has morphed into gender differences that are skewed to the growth of economic activity at the expense our ability to have successful family. Work comes first and last. If the gender history of the last 50 or so years can be described as a war, then neither women nor men have won, or look like winning.

The winner is the economy- not in its original sense of household management but in its abstracted sense of improving Gross Domestic Product. Men and women take prestige from their achievements in the sphere of paid work, leaving being a successful carer a secondary consideration.

Women lose here as well as men. I see my female peers who equalled or bettered me in earning terms during my 20s and early 30s fall behind in their earning power the moment children come along. Of those young women outperforming men in education, outnumbering them in University admissions, how many will still be ahead in earning terms in their 40s and 50s? A number will, and these will be hailed as superwomen if they manage to combine a family life, probably with (low) paid help for the mundane stuff of household management, or be described as an alpha female if they haven't achieved in both spheres. Most, however, will feel a constant sense of struggle and conflict.

The biggest con-trick for both genders though is in relation to the inflationary effect it has had on house prices – requiring two full-time or near full-time incomes to make a house purchase possible. A middle-class preoccupation maybe but one which has consequences for those on lower incomes making even modest aspirations of home ownership out of reach and feeding an aspirational culture which denigrates the option of social housing. Let's remember that we are not talking about an investment in bricks and mortar here but an investment in an idea – the family – that has become beyond the reach the increasing numbers on low incomes.

In short, I think focussing on the achievements of women as part of the reason for why some men struggle, misses the fact that we are all serving something which was meant to serve us: the economy and work.

As for the problem of young men, I find it harder to comment. I am in agreement that I am to a greater degree cocooned from their struggle in my work, not coming into direct contact with the consequences of their exclusion as John and Sandy are. I have interviewed young men on research projects, including one memorably in a young offenders' institution. From these experiences I forged a sense of how the promises of life – a fulfilling job, a house, a family already seemed out of reach. Of their never being given a realistic shot and how they were a hair's breadth from catastrophic realisation. Of how unrealistic the aspirations which replaced them were; often footballers and the life styles of the rich and famous. Manipulated by advertising and celebrity culture to want roles as unlikely as the shipyard or forge workers their great grandfathers might have been. My analysis feels amateur. I'm sure Sandy and John can provide better.

It is maybe true that the adult males these young men came into contact with were few and far between- and often paid to be with them. Which leads me to think about the next steps of this conversation which I assume is to explore ways forward. Do we reinvent gender roles for the world we have created? Or do we reinvent the world so we are less alienated from our human selves and lower the volume on the demands of the workplace? Maybe then, men like myself would not see the lives of young men as abstractly as I currently do, maybe having the time to volunteer and not worry about having my motivations questioned. (Although I do not have a criminal record, I remember the anxiety of applying for my first Disclosure Scotland check. What would their computer throw up? Some misdemeanour of which I was unaware?) My point here is that the disconnection of men like me from the young men who are framed as the problem is a big part of the problem.

Pete

17 AUGUST 2013

We do live in a society where we value commodity above community, where personal happiness seems only to be possible through possessions and status is only measured in relation to work. It is a value system that is accounted only in terms of money.

A consequence of this 'mood music' is reflected in families where their priority is to work to acquire more and more possessions; this means the available time that is left to spend developing and nurturing relationships is significantly reduced. The idea that everyone can have it all was and still is prevalent but the 'all' referred to applies only to physical possessions. A woman can be a wife, a mother and a professional, a man can be a husband, a father and a professional but for many equal effort cannot be given to each of these roles and the roles that are usually given least priority are father and mother. I recall decades ago the expression 'latch key' children used to describe those kids who came home from school to an empty house because mum (usually mum) was out working. This was not intended as a complimentary term and hinted at the disapproval of many to women working, believing that the woman's place was in the home. The women of that time were already engaged in fighting their gender equality war.

I know this is a clumsy analogy but I think, too, relationships have taken characteristics that are strikingly similar to the culture of consumerism. I don't think it's overly dramatic to suggest that relationships now seem to be almost disposable, like products a new model turns up so we just discard the old one and move on. We don't have the time or the opportunity to meet potential partners because we are so busy but we now have dating sites marketed like convenience stores. These sites cater for every taste, professional, middle age, those who work in uniform and many others.

Contraception gave women personal choice and was a hugely significant development that also allowed for family 'planning', which I always assumed was a literal term. This also acknowledged the demands of having a baby and the commitment necessary to raise a child. Now it seems there is little notion of planning to take account of this time and commitment required. Now it is possible to adopt children from around the world and we now hear of 'designer' babies – watch this space! We acquire things now not because we need them or even want them but because we can.

The importance of human relationships in all of this self-interest is lost. I don't think we can reasonably expect our culture to change and perhaps this is just the moment of societal evolution that we are experiencing, it's just our turn, it's our time. Perhaps too constant change is what we do, its life, it's human, so relax it will be fine.

I fully accept our emerging consensus that the challenges are not gender specific, however I do believe that it is vitally important that the role of men is considered with at least as much vigour and determination as the role of women. I don't mean in competition with, or in place of but rather as well as and alongside.

Pete's suggestion that he, and other men like him, should be more visible to those young men living in the most challenging circumstances is true but how that manifests in practice is key. As long as there is a group whose glass is half full giving their time to a group whose glass is half empty then inequality and dependence and difference is maintained.

There is a real danger that as a society we continue to develop professional services to cope with failings in families, relationships and communities. These services never have 'built in' obsolescence and are designed and delivered by people who are not affected by the outcomes. My experience is that with very, very few exceptions, our public services are designed around the deliverer not around the recipient. We value the skills of deliverers and upgrade them constantly so they have certificates and degrees and CPD diplomas but we do not value their human attributes. It's real people that make the difference not skills, strategies or policies, but perhaps this is another subject on its own!

So, while it's great and right that Pete wants to be more visible to these young men and it's not a new idea, how we do that is key, because up until now what we have been doing has not, for the most part, worked.

I think we need more men working in nursery schools, primary schools and secondary schools. We need more men who are doctor's receptionists, nurses, social workers, care workers. We need to value the role of parents, mothers and fathers. We need men to be more vocal about what they believe in. I agree with women that violence against women is intolerable and inexcusable; I agree with women that everyday sexism is unacceptable and I say it out loud.

I believe that rape is about the behavior of men and therefore an issue for men, I believe if we do not stop domestic violence we will never stop violence and I say it out loud.

I also believe the lack of everyday positive male role models and the feminisation of the workforce is having a negative effect on many young boys and men, and I say it out loud.

Not all men are sexist, chauvinist and misogynist and we should not be afraid to speak uncomfortable truths about the particular challenges we face. Inequality and sexism are issues for everyone and that is not always acknowledged but rather seen as a gender war. We must recognise that our response must be inclusive and acknowledged as a shared agenda; that will need people to stick their heads above the parapet and speak the uncomfortable truths out loud.

John

21 AUGUST 2013

The last post has left me thoughtful. I also recognise much of myself in it. Just some points I'd like to respond quickly to.

In terms of the consumerist 'mood music' pushing people to the pursuit of ever more possessions leaving little time for relationships, I'd like to offer a qualification. The decline of community life and the support that came with it has led to the pursuit of material security and possessions to compensate for its decline and general sense of security it offered. I think I have mentioned before how I am childless in part because the level financial security I felt was 'appropriate' for beginning a family was out of my reach until my late 30s. In previous generations, would this have mattered so much? Would people have started families regardless, in part because the social fabric of family and community could compensate the risks of homelessness and job loss? But also because growth and self-development was understood differently?

I'd like to argue that today's relationships (and disagree with me if you like) have become projects which compete with a narrative of personal growth. The 'sensible' thing to do these days being to live a little in your 20s and early 30s, to 'find yourself', to travel or finish other forms of education, often using relationships as the practical experiments in self-finding and then, when fully formed and actualised, cement a long-term relationship (LTR) as icing on the (wedding) cake of successful personhood. To do otherwise is not only considered unfair to yourself but unfair to your potential partner, who is denied a fully rounded adult life partner. Am I being sentimental to think in previous generations, people would start relationships with less thought for their individual growth and recognised that the learning to live through a degree of compromise and a negotiation, of shared times good and hard *was* the process of growth? Adulthood and its relationships was about joining something bigger, a suppression of individuality rather than giving it free reign.

Of course, the dark-side of that oldworld is well known. The drudgery of many people's experiences and for many women, the waste of talents and skills that lay outside what was expected by gender norms. For gay men and women, there was no place out in the open. A society of individuals has liberated many.

Which begs a question? Freed from expectations of gender, why are not more men in caring possessions, primary school teaching or early years work? Is it because the pay is poor and they have little prestige? Men do other jobs with poor pay and little prestige. Is it because the world of certificates and diplomas it represents is better suited to women at the key stage of adolescence and early adulthood? Perhaps the rapidly vanishing apprenticeship model suited many men better. Learning by doing and embedded in relationships of camaraderie. Perhaps many men are simply better suited to clans and communities than a society of individuals. I think some parts of me certainly are.

I agree with John's allusion that an army of well-meaning and certificated men engaging with younger men will not fix 'the problem with men'. But we need find and allow the spaces for all kind of apprenticeships, formal and informal. Which organisations will find the time and inclination to take on the awkward, permanently embarrassed and mumbling teenager I used to be (useless at answering a phone) and teach him how to talk to adults? Who teaches young men to drink in bars where no-one is over 23? Where are the spaces that the informal curriculum used to be taught? Of knowing limits, dealing with conflict and frustrations and even relationships. No doubt couched in the language of outdated chivalry or sexism but experience shared nonetheless. What is missing is not the information but the sharing of the information. The sense that comes from there being people looking out for you, who have experienced your confusion and come through the other side. You can call them 'old farts' when you're with your pals but you might just turn to them another time. Of course few such men today feel qualified to give any advice, in the absence of their certificates.

I'm going away now to think about what we can *do* and signs for *how we would know* when things are improving.

Pete

Hi all,

Two inspiring contributions from John and Pete. I was on my feet shouting 'yes' to each of John's Martin Luther King-esque rallying cries… 'and I say it out loud'. And Pete's insightful speculative critique on the trade-off between personal growth and preparedness for a family – plus his enquiry into the price of certification for the right to give advice. Precisely the reason why I started my charity Working Rite – to give validation to uncertificated non-professional adults in the workplace who are by their very human natures are perfectly capable of mentoring and guiding young people into adulthood and a working future.

I do agree that we live in a commodity-shaped culture but I would quibble (just a wee bit) with John's linking of the drive for possessions with the drive for status. Status per se is not the problem. Ones standing as an adult matters if we are to be effective mentors and elders to the young. Indeed there is in my view a disturbing level of immaturity amongst too many adults. Often adolescents well into adulthood. It is what kind of status and how we measure it that is the question.

My earlier point about History and Balance is important here. What is missing is a sense of ourselves as being on a journey through life right to the bitter end; not just to retirement but quite possibly into the old people's home and for all too many, nightmares like Alzheimer's, with carers young enough to be our great grandchildren behaving like they will never be old themselves. If throughout our lives we rubbed shoulders with the old, learned from the old, indeed learned to respect the old for simply being older – even when they have made bad mistakes and don't use the correct PC language, then maybe our young could grow up to see themselves in the eyes of the dying.

Which leads me to John's point about the professionalisation of services to address the social ills that are designed around the needs of the deliverers. Indeed this point fits well with Pete's question about certification for giving advice rather than acknowledging the 'informal curriculum' of 'old farts'. For me it is because we have lost respect for the past and the old that all skills now need to become certificated and regulated under the vain and unachievable hope that 'bad advice' will never happen.

Perhaps 'learning by doing' is more suited to men and the diploma certificated culture is more suited to women, but I'm not sure. I have listened to some interesting arguments recently making the point that women have been learning fast to 'beat men at their own game' and thus ensure they break into the top jobs. Some say these are in essence patriarchal rules. I think this is too simplistic. Yes, there is a competitive drive in men's work culture. Not in itself bad. Competition gets things done. But what bugs me is the unholy alliance of win/lose winner-takes-all male behaviour combined with feminist social engineering. One where the male warrior instinct is to be defeated and usurped in a paradoxically combative manner rather than re-channelled in a truly adult/elder less adolescent manner. It is as if the past is seen as a purely patriarchal hegemony and that only its total defeat will suffice.

I see the human story as an eternal conveyer belt. New humans dropping on and old ones dropping off every day in perpetuity until the world's end. Each one of us is but a speck in the passage of time. Each generation, each individual soul, tries their best within their own paradigm. To judge those who have gone before en masse as victims or perpetrators in a solely male made conspiracy is pointless. Indeed, it is harmful to our own journey in the present and to those who will follow.

For me this journey is, has been, and always will be, different for males and females. Girls mature differently to boys. Girls become women more obviously – evidenced by their ability to give birth to new life – at least for most of them. Boys become men along a shakier insecure path. Hence the tradition throughout history in all cultures until modern times of rites of passage ceremonies to mark that less obvious transformation. But for both it is a journey where people came before and others will follow.

I believe that to disrespect the role of elders and the lessons, indeed the wisdom, of history is fundamentally damaging to the future of the species – and possibly more harmful to males than for females because, as I've said, women are closer to life's creation. Some years ago I heard that 50 is the new 40. More recently I heard that 60 is the new 40. What bollocks. Eight million people alive in the UK today are predicted to reach 100. What on earth are we trying to do? Cheat death?

In so-called 'traditional societies' the old, the grandparents and great grandparents, are the main carers of children in the first years of life (without being CRB checked) because, they believe, one has just come from the spirit world and the other is about to go there. They have lessons to teach each other. The circularity of life; not the hatred of the aging process. Death is not the enemy, but we now (at least in the professionalised west) live in a society that hates its past and dreads death; a society where the state is seen as the ever ready and eager arbiter of all failings in human relationships; where we imagine that pain and unhappiness can be cured by professional 'early intervention'. Oh dear, oh dear, what have we created?

I say all this while still cheering whole heartedly John's spectacular list of justices to stand for, and moved by Pete's reflections on the hesitancy of prioritising personal growth over just doing. There is no doubt about it that there is a cruelty and overpowering vicious capacity lying deep within the male of the species (I write this as news breaks of yet another gang rape in India). The horror of this and countless horrors on our own doorsteps make me want to reach for a law, an effective piece of schooling, an early intervention, a curfew, a something that the state can do. You may feel that I'm drifting too far from my leftist past, but increasingly I believe that it is human beings – male and female, in all their contradictions and faults, who will do the deep heeling – not the professionals and regulators. And for us as men it is about accessing the unfashionable qualities of courage, honour, strength, leadership and indeed chivalry to make that stand in our ordinary everyday lives – without waiting for a certificate to say we are allowed.

Sandy

26 AUGUST 2014

Dear chaps,

First off, apologies for my silence.

I'm struck that the three most recent contributions have broadened the topic of discussion quite considerably and I can't help feeling that doing so rather undermines the argument (one as you know I'm sceptical of) that there is a crisis specific to men, Scottish or otherwise. If the issues

RELATIONSHIPS AND PROFESSIONALS

now under discussion effect everyone, then not only are we onto a much bigger (and much more challenging) subject area, but it's difficult to see how we relate it only to men or indeed ourselves.

What everyone has touched upon is what Jimmy Reid famously spoke of as 'the Rat Race', and that of course means both male and female rats, although of course the drudgery of everyday life can take its toll on them in different ways. Could it be that the closing of the gender gap when it comes to personal and professional lives has produced downsides as well as up? Or does that make me sound hopelessly old fashioned? I remember encountering a middle-aged Republican gentleman in Birmingham, Alabama, who told me that society (by which he meant traditional family life) was about to collapse because in the 1960s women had been encouraged to pursue careers and sleep with whoever they liked. I instinctively contradicted him, for it struck me as an absurd thing to say. But equally that social revolution – which I might add came a little late even for someone of my mother's generation and class – has undoubtedly eroded traditional male dominance in certain areas and thus inevitably increased anxiety. In that sense I agree with John, but there's a difference between wanting to reverse that and managing the transition better.

A few random, and quite personal, observations from the past few weeks. I've never encountered homophobia (beyond low-level sniggering and discomfort among associates) but a few months ago my partner and I were on Sark (an autonomous island within the Bailiwick of Guernsey, it's all very complicated) and were walking (not hand in hand or even that close to each other) on a coastal path when a group of lads clearly on a stag do passed us on their bikes going in the other direction. One of them looked at us and chirped 'Alright gays' and then carried on. Initially I wasn't sure I'd heard him right, but when it sunk in we were both quite shaken. This sounds melodramatic; the feeling did not last long and it was an innocuous remark delivered in obvious high spirits, but nevertheless someone had clocked me (accurately, of course) as gay and for some reason I resented it. On reflection, I know why. Although open about my sexuality I like being what is generally referred to as 'straight-acting' (although it's obviously not an act), I suppose because on a mischievous level I like people assuming I'm straight. So that 'Alright, gays' cut through that and essentially questioned my perception of myself as quite masculine. In the context of everything I've said previously about my generation being more relaxed about such things, which was obviously quite an interesting response.

Recently I also revisited some old haunts from my childhood and school-days, and it left me rather melancholy. Not because I hankered after those days: I don't, generally speaking I did not enjoy my early years or my education (such as it was), but because cycling around Lochend, Restalrig and Leith (all in Edinburgh) I was struck by how cut off it is from the rest of the city. Not geographically of course, none of those places is far from the city centre, but in terms of class, mobility, income and, I guess, gender issues. As I've touched on before, part of me considers hand-wringing about masculinity and the crisis of the Scottish male as little more than irrelevant, middle-class preoccupations, first-world problems if you like. I know that's unfair, but it's an impression that crops up again and again. That's obviously paradoxical, because for people lower down the Rat Race getting to grips with all those things would probably do them a lot of good, but I doubt many such discussions will actually take place.

Despite all this I still find it difficult to think of my life, my past and my future in terms of being a man. Perhaps, as I've also said before, it's because being gay blurs the lines (ever so slightly), and perhaps because I'm a bit younger than the rest of you. I guess I'm saying I have contra-dictory views, as will be clear from the paragraphs above!

Cheers,

David

Dear All,

I agree with David that we have developed our thinking and discussions to the stage where we have altered the main plank of our challenge, 'a crisis for masculinity'. We are describing now a crisis of relationships, a crisis of living together, a crisis of community and perhaps even a generational crisis.

David's latest has made me think that in trying to define what it is we should do we should take care and not presume that there is a problem with a solution and we have managed to define both. I think when we are each typing our contributions we should have in mind exactly who we are thinking about. David is using very personal experiences, we have all done that, but I am also thinking about young men, young women and families that I have encountered in my professional life and I am certain Sandy is too.

To be clear I think the transition in relationships is having a negative impact on some men, not all men. My view is that it is not an absolute necessity to have a positive male role model in the life of every boy. But for many boys there is a lack of any kind of role model except negative ones. For many young boys having a positive male role model is the difference between living a reasonable life or living a difficult life and dying young, having never experienced hope. The connection I am making to ALL men is because like women and feminism, I believe we should stand together and do what we can for each other try to give voice to those who have none, to level the playing field to acknowledge that it is just not fair.

Many of the young men I have encountered have no sense of belonging to anything. They see no future for themselves in any context, no prospects of a job, no prospects of a family. When we think of status they have none except what they establish for themselves on the street, through fighting, drinking and rebelling. There is no sense of redemption for these men, gather a couple of previous convictions when you're 17 or 18 and you can forget getting a job. Get a scar on your face and you're unlikely to get a job at Malmaison.

I have met some incredible young men who have turned very difficult lives around; for them there was usually some significant person and some particular event. Reaching the bottom of the hole and saying 'I've had enough'. At this exact same time they need to encounter the right person willing and able to help them. Right now for the vast majority of young men descending into their own personal abyss there is no one to say 'stop, I care about you and I can help you', we thought this job could be done by professionals, it can't.

I was compelled to reach the conclusion that men were in crisis because of what I saw and experienced as a cop. I saw feckless young men who did stupid things, who didn't care about themselves, who had no hope. There was and is a common thread that connects these young men, the lack of positive male role models in their lives. Other young men look to sporting heroes or public figures but for these young men these are not adequate substitutes. Their mums all loved them but could not cope with them. Their early years were usually chaotic. I then connected what I saw in these young men with what for me is a significant shift in relationships. I presumed therefore that the presence of a positive role model would make it all better. I am not sure that I have changed my mind in this regard. Perhaps it's my age and life experience that has me jumping onto a solution for a problem before I have given a great deal of thought of to the problem. Perhaps, too, the need to blame something, like feminism was too tempting.

Perhaps the solution to this challenge is not to wish a turning back of the clock to a time when it seems fine, when in fact it wasn't, but rather as David suggests we should try to manage the transition better. I don't think we can do this on our own, men I mean, I think we will need to make the case that there is an issue and it is an issue has implications for everyone. The war that has been waged by feminism to balance real gender inequality is ongoing with some progress made but still much more to be done. In these times do we think we can make the case that women need to pay attention to the role of men; I suspect we might find it difficult to enlist the wholehearted support of women in this particular endeavor.

Do we think the young women of this generation think consciously of gender equality or are they content with their lot as it is, at least for the most part? Are the majority of young men generally quite happy with their world too, 43 per cent single person households in Glasgow, absent dads, fewer responsibilities? What will happen to this next generation who are being brought up without fathers being present in their life?

Sandy I think I understand your issue around status but how are we to frame status in the context you describe? Is it to be defined by material wealth, intellect, class, gender, professional position, societal position? I can remember when status was afforded to the 'man of the house' the 'bread winner,' when being a police officer had a status, perhaps even a moral authority, we do after all still police by consent. Teachers say their status is eroded, politicians too. Could it be a more cynical public or is personal status no longer of any importance unless it can be equated to wealth and possession, the Rich List. Even journalists had some status.

Status is not something that is bestowed or awarded it is in part defined by the norms of the times, of society's norms, of community norms. The gang fighter, 'the leader off' has status in the gang but will probably be unable to read or write and will never have job and die prematurely.

There is also a generational dimension to all of this, which is interesting. There seems to be unwillingness from some of my generation to give the next generation the space to be different; is this a response to and fear of change? Is their status and power associated with age? And is it so different with this generation? I recall it was like this when I was in my teens. When I joined the Police, I was 21, I walked the beat with a man who had been on the beach at Normandy on D-Day and my first sergeant was at Arnheim. They thought I was very different from them and said so. They also advised me, coached me, encouraged me and tutored me. I should also say that my mentor is a retired Royal Marine Major General, he and I have many things in common, perhaps some things that some would describe as 'old fashioned' but nonetheless important; a sense of service, integrity and loyalty.

I still think the nature of relationships and the role of men is the challenge. For some men it is fine and is having little impact, but for some it is having a huge impact. Young boys who have no-one to model on, no behaviour to copy, no role to aspire to. Such boys gather with other young boys who have the same challenges, this is only possible because we have usefully placed them together living side by side.

I know this does not go anywhere near answering Pete's question to think of what to do and if it works what it might look like.

I know that this is a wicked problem and when we try to fix one part of it another part will get worse. This is evidenced clearly when we think of the challenge as one of relationships. For some the current direction of travel is great and viewed as progress, which it is, but as

David suggests we need to manage the change better. We need to understand the consequences of some trends and actions.

Perhaps we should keep it simple, if we think some young men lack good male role models, let's do something practical about it and create some way of supporting young boys to become men. Sandy is already doing this and there are others but it's not to sufficient scale; as always it's not the plan or strategy that is the problem its people and attitudes.

Directly connecting the plight of disenfranchised young men to the progress of gender equality, even if we could, is incendiary and it is unlikely to help anyone.

John

CHAPTER SIX

Lads, Laddism and a More Equal Society

3 SEPTEMBER 2013

I'm beginning to understand the crisis of masculinity as a crisis of absences. An absence from the gender debate is one such. Perhaps because the framing of the gender debate locates it away from areas of traditional masculine comfort. Laden as it is with a crippling sensitivity around the wrongs men inflict on others, men as well as women. It has left us unable to find a way to enter the debate constructively, other than apologetically or as caveman. Extremes prevail. On the one hand, delicately learning the language of inclusivity and gender neutrality so that nervousness around how we express ourselves prevents us expressing ourselves. Or more recently the terrifying emergence of campus 'Lads' (the caveman) devoid of any of the knowing, eyebrows raised, post-feminist – 'we all know this is wrong so we can laugh about it' version of the 1990s laddism. Bear in mind that this earlier form of the Lad had a female ally, the Laddette, who drank and smoked as comrade and equal to young men and has been implicated in the rise in female alcohol related harm.

Looking back at this moment in cultural history- perhaps a more English moment than a Scottish one, 1990s laddism felt like a potentially corrective moment and its relationship to the voice of the working class male was important. The '80s demonised the culture of working class men, with football hooliganism and industrial strife synonymous in media representations of their world. New forms of expressivity through music and club-culture, the middle classes falling back in love with football and finally, a sense of new hope after a long, long winter of Tory rule changed the climate offering new ways to enact being a working class man. Also, of course, a new breed of working class male made good was arriving in the agenda setting salons of the Sunday supplements. However, somewhere along the way the 'lad' became another cartoon representation of working class masculinity. Rather than a Jarvis or a Manic, we got the Gallachers and a Beckham as a lasting legacy to represent young working class males. The former embraced hedonism and a never apologise cockiness as the way forward, the latter at his best when he chose not to speak, standing for a representation of what can be achieved through shopping.

I don't know enough about contemporary music and fashion to know whose re-shaping masculinity today. My knowledge stops somewhere around the time of Mike Skinner's The Streets and therefore I'll bow out gracefully from attempting to offer some sources of change for today's younger men, for fear of sounding like an embarrassing uncle dancing at a wedding disco.

What my excursion does say however is that if we do not define masculinities for ourselves, others will do it for us. For some reason, masculinity has become a common sense concept, the sort that doesn't get unpacked and reanalysed enough. Yes, we've been doing it in these exchanges but it hasn't always felt comfortable and sometimes it has felt a distinctly un-masculine exercise. Like a big part of being masculine is knowing what it is and just being it. Like being funny or being cool, analysis is its mortal enemy.

This conversation has reinforced my belief in the social and cultural aspects of masculinity. That it is not all down to genetics or we are prisoners to behaviours and outlooks that proved successful when our ancestors hunted mammoths. Yes, there is an archaeology of previous modes of being, previous ways of being a man, layered on top of each other. This is why scratch the surface and a semblance of the warrior or hunter may be revealed. In much of our discussion we have focussed on two historically closer roles; of industrial worker and (nuclear) family man. Roles which now have extra layers on top, of post-industrial worker and of men in a world where there are changed gender roles not only around family but also possible around reproduction. Public conversation of masculinity must focus on how these are being made sense of and shaping what it is to be a man as much as how we deal with the remains of outmoded forms, no longer useful. It is the behaviours which become redundant not the people practising them.

So what would I like to see? Of course, I would like to see the presence of more men in the gender debate, particularly working class men. Perhaps setting up the 'crisis' of masculinity head-to-head with feminism is not the place the start. It invites defensive positioning and can position feminism as an antithesis of masculinity rather than its rescuer. For rescuer it can be. Forcing an examination of ways of being so long taken for granted as to be assumed natural, highlighting the fluid and malleable ways in which gender is constructed for us. Showing us that we can change the categories so many have been forced to live by. Why not recognise that feminism has the analytical power to unpack the subjugation of men? A subjugation brought by a limited repertoire of roles many find uncomfortable and past their usefulness.

As feminists have pointed out, being a man has historically been seen as the default position. I have understood this abstract statement more through these exchanges. Being a man 'just is'. A synonym for person-hood, merged in there with my individuality, my class, my sexuality, my age cohort, my white Anglo ethnic self. My masculinity is both obvious and elusive. This is a real barrier to conversation around gender and finding the words to describe what is assumed to be self-evident.

What I have learned most through these exchanges however is the absence of men in the lives of other, younger men. This is not new. The emotionally absent yet physically present male of family life is a figure familiar to many. But even in these circumstances, a role model, no matter how flawed (and perhaps role models should have flaws) is available. Let's also remember that these relationships offer two way learning. Young teaching old about the world they are entering and creating, providing feedback for ways of being that are losing their usefulness. Perhaps also role modelling for men takes place in the silences. So familiar is the story of years of poor communication, of estrangement between fathers and sons for resolution to be found not in embraces and loquacious reunion but in quiet acceptance of differ-ence. A story so recognisable it must contain a deeper truth. It is in these moments of acceptance and reconciliation, that the skills which would make for a better world are learned and understood.

These mundane and familiar stories need to be heard and discussed. Also needing to be heard are the stories of men dealing with change when that change cuts right to the heart of their masculinity. Perhaps it is only here that we can grasp masculinity and set it apart from the other ways of being we inhabit. Stories of men dealing with transition from being an industrial worker to service sector job seeker. From doting father to estranged, absent father. From gang-member to job seeker or apprentice. From provider to pensioner. How masculinity is reconstructed in these moments so that it still makes sense in changed circumstances has learning for all of us.

Pete

15 SEPTEMBER 2013

Pete's latest contribution seems to me to get to the heart of what our exchanges have exposed, at least for me. We all came to this conversation convinced to varying degrees of certainty that masculinity was in crisis or at least was changing to such an extent that it required examination and discussion to better understand it. We each had considered personal views, some shared, that the role of men in 21st century was so unclear, so changed and ill-defined that it was having a serious and negative impact on a whole suite of societal problems including violence, alcohol, employment and relationships. It hadn't really occurred to me that since I have never 'studied' sociology or anthropology or economics or psychology or philosophy, my arrival at this conclusion was founded solely on what my idea of being a man was and indeed that this idea of manhood had been formed from my personal experience. What's even worse is that I presumed that everyone, at least every man, would understand and identify wholly with my conclusion.

I realise now that this process is so obviously flawed that I am embarrassed to openly acknowledge my failure to recognise its weakness or even to raise it at such an advanced point in our discussions, it serves little purpose other than to perhaps frustrate you all, apologies for this. David has helped focus my thoughts with his scepticism about the narrowness of our original premise, he is right, the issue is far broader and involves everyone in society. Pete's suggestion that that there is a generational component seems also to make sense and if this is all about how society has changed then perhaps as David suggests we should be trying to manage the transition better.

I have become convinced through our exchanges that the role(s) of men need to be discussed and examined not in an exclusive self-serving way and not in a way that focuses blame but rather in a way that helps everyone, men and women, cope equally well with the challenges. Further, this needs to be done with the same vigour, bravery and honesty that have been applied to the challenges as they affect women.

Having said all this, I do think it is important as Pete suggests that we think more about what to do. I personally thought the most apparent and clear impact of changing role for men or transition was in relation to the role of fathers, extending that to include positive role models. If I wasn't sure of the direct link with all of these problems I was absolutely certain of the causal relationship; I remain absolutely certain of this causal relationship.

No matter how hard I try, I find that I have been framing my thinking almost exclusively within the feminist agenda, seeing the challenges faced by men as coming about as a direct consequence of the changes in the role of women, if not entirely then at least in part. This is not to say that I don't agree with that cause because I do, and in many respects I envy the unifying nature of the feminist 'cause'. It is something men do not seem to have. It is a single unifying movement that focuses attention, creates consensus and encourages active responses.

As an example of the effectiveness of this 'cause' I note how often we now seem to have public comment and an increasing outcry at the notion of all male panels on some political TV programmes. Yet, men say little about the lack of male teachers in nurseries and schools. There is always comment about the objectification of women, with a woman's worth being measured in terms of how they look or what they wear. Yet, in advancing the feminist cause, men are usually portrayed in stereotypical negative terms. Perhaps men need to define their own role in society or at least challenge that which we are not.

I am on the board of a charity and as part of their fund raising programme they have run several ladies lunches. These lunches usually have a male comedian who is also gay, make-up demonstrations, nail bar and a group known as 'butlers in the buff'; naked men who wear aprons and serve at the lunch. These men are all young and physically attractive. At a recent meeting of the board the men present raised the idea of some similar event they could organise just for men. We found it difficult to come with an idea that wasn't like a stag night or sportsman's dinner and all suggestions involved drink, the other board members are senior medical consultants.

I suppose my point is that this is an issue for everyone and requires collaboration not division.

In relation to what we might usefully do, I think work is at the heart of all of this. When I meet young men in some of the most deprived areas of Scotland or the young men in Polmont or Barlinnie, what's missing in their personal history is a positive male role model and what is lacking in their envisioned future is a lack of work and with it the absence of purpose and meaning. What's usually always present is alcohol and violence. The lives of these men are at the extreme end of negative outcomes and while they are a minority they do reflect a significant proportion of young men today; they will usually also be fathers. All of us must have some sense of worth or purpose or a notion that we belong to a society or a community and that our contribution no matter what, is meaningful, otherwise who cares what happens.

The fight for these young men is to be forgiven and then accepted and treated fairly. Today a young man with a couple of previous convictions will be precluded immediately from getting a job. Previous convictions are first and foremost not very reliable as an indicator of character and they only require that you get caught doing something that is illegal; the police only catch the feckless and the stupid. I know young men who have previous convictions for disorder, not violence and not dishonesty, yet they are sifted from job selections even if the job is emptying bins. This should be our cause or at least part of it.

Women have children, only women can have children, so in many respects a woman's sense of worth and purpose can be fulfilled through motherhood. Women can now have successful professional careers and be mothers and while I do accept that this is not true for every woman and every career or job it is true for the majority. The differentiation I would make is along similar lines to that David described in relation to generation and class.

The changing job market has seen the type and volume of jobs that were exclusive to men decrease dramatically. Moreover women have fought to ensure they have access to all jobs, even those that would have previously been seen as 'male only'. For many young men brought up experiencing only the negative influence of adult men in their life and the life of their mothers it must be a very confusing world.

It is true that for many young men the transition or social change we have been discussing will have little direct effect on their lives, perhaps even no effect at all. These young men will have the protection of parents, place, education and opportunity. But for many the impact will be their feeling and experiencing that this is the only way of life for them, with little aspiration, little sense of belonging. What is even worse is that this feeling of alienation is being passed from one generation to the next, with each generation further reinforcing the hopelessness.

I would say also that for many young women, like the young men I speak of, the notion of what is possible is severely limited and the feminist agenda to them will have very little relevance to their everyday lives. Their life histories will be very similar to the young men I'm speaking of, their futures too are shared.

This is an issue for everyone and if we agree that what we really need to do is manage the transition better then that's where we should start. It's about equality.

Best,

John

16 SEPTEMBER 2013

Dear chaps,

I'm very struck by John's concluding words: 'It's about equality.'

Indeed it is, and I agree with much of what he says about casting it more widely than just 'men' (and, indeed, 'Scottish men'). I also feel humbled; I hadn't expected that my thoughts would have such an effect on (at least) John's approach to this topic.

It's left me wondering what the masculine form of feminism might be. Masculinism? Although having just typed that, a quick Google search reveals it (obviously) isn't an original thought. The OED defines it as:

'Advocacy of the rights of men; adherence to or promotion of opinions, values, etc., regarded as typical of men; (more generally) anti-feminism, machismo', although surely it doesn't necessarily need to be 'anti' anything. Political scientists have also got to work, with the splendidly named Georgia Duerst-Lahti distinguishing between the two terms, with masculism being more associated with the early gender egalitarian days of the men's movement, while masculinism is refers to patriarchy and its ideology. Gerry will no doubt know about all of this, but it's new to me. But then, as I've already said, I've never taken a particularly close interest in such things.

As in history, there is nothing new under the sun.

David

16 SEPTEMBER 2013

Dear all,

I recently saw an advert for board members for Scottish Women's Aid, it said only women were eligible to apply. I contacted Lily Greenan who is CEO of SWA; I said that I didn't want to cause any issues but that I would be interested in becoming a director on her board. I get on very well with Lily otherwise I would not have contemplated the contact and the question, she advised that the constitution of the SWA stated that only women could be members of the board. She did concede that perhaps we were nearing time when that policy should be revisited.

I am relating this story since we have been discussing 'masculinism' and feminism and to give some hope that maybe we could make some headway in our consensual ambitions.

Best wishes,

John

16 SEPTEMBER 2013

This thing on masculinism.

I believe boys are more drawn to risk than girls when growing up. When I read John's reflections of the young men who are probably excluded forever because they got caught and convicted of something I am enraged.

Pete recently wrote of the certificating drive of the professions and wondered whether that was a feminine trait. Well, I would add the risk assessment risk reduction culture.

I believe that it is natural for women to seek safety for others. A laudable intention some might say, but it denies the nature of the male. Boys test the world around them when charting their clumsy pathway through adolescence. They take risks and get into trouble. And this is the way it has to be. If we create a civil society that requires an unblemished journey then we automatically exclude many boys simply by their gender. Now that is prejudice. CRB check, declarations of previous offences, risk assessments. This is the world of mothers taking care of the children. All very fine and worthwhile. But we are simply not understanding boys. And because the social professions are so overwhelmingly dominated by the feminine we have created and institutionalised discrimination AGAINST males. Where is the sexism now?

Recently in my own charity, a male worker informed us that his CRB check was likely to reveal a past criminal conviction when he was 19 years old for affray and aggravated assault. When I informed a funder who demanded to know about the problem, her response was say we should suspend him immediately pending the outcome of the check. This funder said they were concerned for the reputation for the Working Rite brand. I agreed. I would indeed be concerned about the reputation of the Working Rite brand... as HYPOCRITES!! How on earth could we lay claim to being a charity that supports wayward youngsters and have a recruitment policy that says 'don't bother coming to us in 20 years' time looking for a job'?

So long as I am in charge of Working Rite there will not be a requirement to declare any convictions in your application form (CRB checks after an offer of a job for child sex abuse excepted). Also, no application for any job in our charity, no matter how senior, requires any qualification as a requirement. These measures are the best small steps that I can take to ensure that older men who once were young and made silly choices do not get discriminated against in later life so far as Working Rite is concerned by a seemingly well-meaning but fundamentally prejudiced anti-male, feminine professional hegemony.

There you have it. I've let off steam. This stuff makes my blood boil.

Sandy

18 SEPTEMBER 2013

In response to David's search for a term to describe the male form of feminism, I, too, have thought about this previously and have always drawn a blank, often mildly embarrassed by the ridiculousness or scope for misinterpretation in resultant terms ('masculinism' being a good example). To be honest I have always thought 'gender' to be a workable term for exploring the issues of male identity. Feminism was not only a movement which promoted the rights of women but was also in the vanguard of unpacking the idea of gender as an enactment, something we *do* rather than inescapably *are*, in which male and female play-off and define one another consciously and unconsciously. Although this works for me, I can see it is a nightmare sell more generally. Perhaps we should not worry about giving it a name. Reflection on why some men have their disadvantage compounded at an early age by the forces of either law and order or risk averse bureaucracy needs to be maintained within the inequalities debate. This is clear from both John's and Sandy's posts.

John says that the Police only catch the 'feckless and the stupid'. Can I add that they are also more likely to catch the poor? This is because they have more resource allocated to deprived areas because of the higher crime rates found there, particularly the more visible street-based variety rather than the murkier white collar or insurance fraud variety. John, I know you are one of Scotland's biggest advocates for young men from deprived backgrounds and your work has improved the lives of many of these men and their families. But let's be clear, it is society (in whose interest the Police act) not feminism that is criminalising these young men for often minor first time indiscretions; drinking or urinating in a public place, possession of illegal substances, affray, vandalism and other forms of anti-social behaviour.

So, it seems all are calling for more opportunities for risk and expressiveness in society. Currently denied, opportunities are pushed to the margins where the hazards to life chances are greatly increased; through drugs and intoxication or the excitement of running with a team, stealing a car or tagging. Having the capability to take risks to explore one's boundaries should be framed as a 'Right' as well as a 'rite'. What's absent from the inequalities perspective is recognition of how risk aversion (and not a more nuanced risk 'awareness') pushes young men (and some women) further to the margins. So one action it seems is to be vigilant to maintain space for risk for our young men; rule breaking without the life threatening consequences of bureaucracy.

That's a society I'd be proud to live in.

Pete

18 SEPTEMBER 2013

Pete, I think your observations on the policing of the poor are very accurate. The recent reporting of stop search strategies is an excellent example of this.

The police like other agencies do act in the interests of 'society 'Our society made 'anti-social behaviour' illegal through the mechanisms of government and law making. Did anyone think that by making something illegal it would be sorted? If it was that easy we should make cancer illegal. Criminal Justice is the service of last resort.

Governments can make laws and spend taxes and they are not very enthusiastic about the latter. About three years ago, I spoke at the Law Society dinner and uncovered the following in some research for that speech. Between 1945 and the 1980s, this country's lawmakers created five new Criminal Justice Bills – that is one per decade. Between 1997 and 2010 this country's lawmakers created 4,300 new offences – that is 28 per month.

So, the Police can only enforce or enact legislation that is created by our legislature and if governments legislate against the poor and disadvantaged then the natural outcome will be that the police are seen to focus in on the poor. We are an instrument of the state but within criminal justice it is the legitimate role of the courts to protect the individual citizens from the worst excesses of the state. They don't.

It seems too that in creating 'others' to blame society absolves itself of any personal responsibility. It's the young who behave badly, it's the idle who won't work, it's the feckless who are a drain on public resources. An example at the moment is Minimum Unit Pricing for alcohol. If we frame this around reducing the alcohol intake of young people or alcoholics or poor people then the argument is obviously flawed, however if we consider that we all drink too much and that there is too much availability and that it is too cheap then the argument for MUP is sound.

I agree, too, it is not feminism that has criminalised the young men I spoke of, but if they had a voice and influence that was the equal of the feminist voice maybe the law makers would enact laws that favour them instead of victimising them. Further, having singled them out for discriminatory treatment through the enactment and enforcement of primary legislation we then continue to punish them by creating further legislation that denies them any hope of rehabilitation. This not only affects the individual but also their families, their children, their community because we have conveniently cordoned them off away from the rest of us. Check out the postcodes in Barlinnie, then check out the generational connection.

It is not only national policy and lawmakers that perpetuate this discrimination. The application of the licensing laws is the statutory responsibility of local authorities. How many off sales outlets are there per head of population in Easterhouse compared to Milngavie? Alcohol's link to violence is well documented so surely it cannot be a surprise to anyone that there are more arrests in Easterhouse for drink related offending than in Milngavie? That's not a policing strategy.

Easterhouse does not have a community centre. It has a shopping centre, with pawn shops, betting shops, Bright House, payday lenders all licensed by local authorities, how many in Milngavie? If you do not have a bank account and have to pay for your electricity by using a pay-as-you-go meter in your home, the charge per unit is far higher than you or I pay.

As I said at the end of my last contribution, this is about equality.

John

94

Dear chaps,

We seemed to have strayed into crime and punishment!

I am glad the conversation has steered on to this more holistic territory as it matches my general thinking on this. As you know from my earlier contributions, I feel whatever problems that exist with 'maleness' or 'masculinity' are vastly outweighed by the biggest issue that faces the UK, the US and many other 'developed' Western countries: inequality. Tackle that and arguably everyone – male and female – will benefit, and the means of tackling that problem ought to be preoccupying us all. If you haven't already, I urge you to read Joseph Stiglitz's recent book *The Price of Inequality*. Unlike *The Spirit Level*, it hasn't generated much 'middle-class excitement', but it's an important work which (incidentally) has been completely misrepresented by certain figures in the Scottish Government.

Talking of the Scottish Government, I was very struck the other day that Alex Bell, Alex Salmond's former senior policy adviser, used an article in *The Guardian* to criticise the Yes Scotland campaign for not thinking holistically about the challenges facing every Western economy, ie worn out economic models, inequality and demographic time-bombs. Rather, he said, those advocating a 'yes' vote gave the impression that an independent Scotland would simply 'tweak' the status quo, which of course would barely tackle any of the above. On that point he was bang on. Few are prepared to think about this in any depth, but what else could be more important?

Of course, this would have a gender dimension, as well as an age one, sexuality and so on, but I can't help feeling we all ought to get our priorities right!

David

20 SEPTEMBER 2013

Dear all,

The recent intervention by Alex Bell (a former Scottish Government adviser) in the luke-warm referendum debate has introduced a degree of maturity and urgency to those particular proceedings. I hope it can contribute to changing the character of the dialogue that so far has been short on inspiration. We cannot afford the referendum to be about short –term promises; the timescale evoked in the idea of nation-hood goes beyond the usual electoral cycles. Perhaps we are poor at encouraging our politicians to be candid in such timescales, instead preferring to judge them and their credibility on growth figures and other short-term deliverables. Neither of the outcomes to the referen-dum indicate (at least not without further explanation) the solution to the issues we have been discussing. One dimension of the crisis being the urgent need to re-imagine the social contract between individuals, communities and society in fundamentally changed times.

A re-imagining of society is necessary, amongst other pressing reasons, so as older people we can all thrive and not just survive. What do the problems we have identified in these exchanges say about how life might look like early years of our new society, independent or not?

We have touched strongly on the theme of male redundancy. Not just from paid work but from a positive societal role. The demographic/austerity crisis demands we reconsider the idea of life-course and in particular old age and our relationships to work. Rather than seeing old age as a period of decline, coming after our economically produc-tive years, we have to reconsider the notion of productivity to include those roles for which we are *not* paid to do. In doing so we can re-im-agine the later years as a time of growth rather than decline. We can also re-imagine our ideas of national wealth. Could it also be used to re-imagine manhood and masculinity?

All of us in these exchanges have indicated how central a foundation our ability to get paid to do something is to our sense of who we are; to our manhood. Yet, on account of where the UK has chosen to position itself in the global economy, meaningful *paid* work remains further away from those in the most disadvantaged communities than ever before. So it is a paradox that those of us lucky enough to have paid work will probably have to do it later into life than any generation before. The on-going crisis should force a re-evaluation of the place of paid work across the entirety of our lives. Paying more attention to the other activities such as volunteering and being good citizen, community member, family member or even friend. All are activities that produce numerous forms of value – from the wellbeing to those engaged in it to the cost savings in terms of the welfare and health spend in the prevention of long term mental and physical health conditions.

Communities are stronger as a result and much of our conversation has highlighted how such activities have been colonised by certification and regulation, pushing men to the margins in the process.

How we achieve this recalibration of economic and non-economic forms of value is beyond the scope of this dialogue. But for all of us, it can offer scope to mentor, support and be visible in all spheres. Hopefully, it can offer new and valuable roles and offer new narratives of meaning for all, with all men included.

Pete

22 SEPTEMBER 2013

I make a plea to keep this simple and not over think it, a complex problem does not always require an equally complex solution; particularly true if we want to actually do something about these problems.

We have shifted our focus considerably from our starting point, from a crisis of masculinity to a crisis that affects us all. I wonder if any committed and active feminists see their challenge in the same way. I understand that the feminist movement acknowledge that men have to be part of the solution to 'their' problems, but that's different from identifying challenges that are common to both sexes – and it's a huge step away from mutually-agreed responses.

Like Pete I think we could usefully consider what actions we might need – mentoring, or the broader concept about the visibility of men has been mentioned, as has work and relationships. Given that our early exchanges focused very much on masculinity and feminism I think it might be worthwhile to try to create some dialogue to unite or order our thinking on the basis of gender, challenges that are shared irrespective if they are the cause or the solution. Violence against women is about men's behaviour and is corrosive for both sexes. Feminism can take the concept of guil by association too far, violence against women harms and victimises women, all women, but it also diminishes men, all men.

Our society seems to value commodity above community and we have embraced this notion with such conviction that we seem now to be living in a constant state of dissatisfaction. In our jobs we always need new challenges, promoted, more money; in our relationships many seem to be constantly on the lookout for something new or someone better; we want new things, cars, houses, possessions. Our human inclination to conform has us all joining in. This fuels and intensifies inequality but we don't care because self is the most important driver, we are selfish.

What key elements, behaviours or character traits might we agree are unique to men and define our masculinity? I recall a group of us once made an unsuccessful attempt to write a ten-point manifesto for men, despite our failure then I think the process of considering what each of us think defines masculinity would give some clue to the important elements of the 'transition' David speaks of. I suspect too it will highlight the generational and experiential distinctions and differences between each of us.

Empathy seems a good trait to start off on. It is often referred to as a feminine trait and, a bit like nurture, it's not something that men do. Perhaps that was true, I suspect not, but I believe there are signs that human empathy is receding as a valued human trait in women too.

The number of TV programmes that are about bullying is very worrying. These progammes offer fame as a highly valued 'commodity' that is available to anyone and everyone with just a little talent. We then enjoy laughing at them when they fail. This works because the show's organisers encourage prospective 'stars' to go in front of large theatre audiences or huge TV audiences where they are immediately exposed as having no talent, then we laugh at them; and it's not just men who are laughing. It's bullying.

The advent and use of social media has added a whole new and worrying dimension to bullying. Girls and women bully other girls and women relentlessly.

The use and abuse of alcohol is a huge challenge, particularly in Scotland. The increase in alcohol consumption is most obvious in women's intake but the challenge is another the sexes share.

The feminisation of the workforce is another shared challenge. Could we articulate some shared challenges? Would doing this help equality? Speaking of criminal justice, rape and pornography, we have made little mention of any these subjects, bad for men.

John

1 OCTOBER 2013

When asked to take part in this discussion, my initial thoughts were not with a pressing need to explore and address a crisis of masculinity or a crisis of men. I anticipated an exploration of how being a man has morphed over the decades, of how different enactments of masculinity have become possible, of some of the things we've lost but also what men and society have gained and what this made possible for a future Scotland. I anticipated a context of the referendum debate as an opportunity to forge new cultural relationships around gender. I now feel naïve about my original position, a little optimistic and of misidentifying my own experience for that of all men in Scottish society.

I was not unaware of the problems that beset men in contemporary Scotland. I knew of the higher suicides rates for men, that the lower life expectancies found across Scotland are led by men, I knew about gang violence, of higher rates of conviction and of intergenerational unemployment and a loss of role for many men. I understood these as issues that affected men but not a crisis exclusively 'of men'. I've been forced to confront my initial position in the discussion. I have however, been left uncertain of whether there is or isn't a set of social problems that are grounded in societally based inequalities against men. What the arguments and perspectives of my fellow discussants has convinced me of is of a number of trends which effect all in society are experienced in particular ways by a large number of men for which there isn't an adequate language to describe and formulate actions.

One of these trends is the seismic adjustment made in the character of work. Unemployment, precariousness, de-skilling, re-skilling, races to the bottom and alienation from paid work are trends effecting men and women. Whereas, rightly, there is a legal, moral and technical framework to monitor women's progress in the workplace, in the achievement (or not) of rights, pay and equality, there has not been a particular moral lens applied to tackling in the in social injustice of men who have not shared in economic gains. Many men have gained in the transition to a service economy and reap the benefits not just materially but also culturally in taking advantage of more fluid identities. So have many women. However, many, men and women, have also failed to gain and have fallen behind rather that benefitted from opportunity, it's just that we are better at describing the ways in which one gender is held back than the other.

I am now closer to accepting a clear developmental gender difference in young men's greater propensity for risk taking. The shift in how important socialisation activity is provided (by apprenticeships of both formal and informal kinds) has moved learning about the world from the sphere of the interpersonal to a more formal, professional realm. This may not suit many young men and can compound early educational failures. It also prevents older men from having an important role. I have also been convinced of the real issue of the absence of role models for boys, in families, the community, schools and services. Could we imagine a job advert for a Primary school teacher which specified male applicants only, on the basis of their current absence within the teaching staff? Would this use of legislative methodology actually improve the situation? It seems contradictory to use the very thing we are bemoaning as the proposed solution. Still, it is a thought I might not have had before these discussions.

Ultimately though, I have been convinced more than ever of the need for opportunities for meaningful paid work and the experiences that come with it. For all. By 'meaningful' I mean work which allows a sense of being part of something greater than one's self, of having an impact and part to play in the world, of mattering. In the absence of this, unobtainable caricatures of respect, wealth and status can distort a sense of what is important. For young men these can lead to the dark side of masculine identity: violence and gender-based violence, crime and decreased mental wellbeing.

As for my initial position and anticipation of discussion of the different ways in which we do masculinity, manhood or whatever we choose to call it, I am glad to have been shaken from my comfortable position.

Scotland badly requires a basis of solidarity we can all buy into. A shared view of what kind of journey we are collectively on and shapes our understanding of social justice. I think some of the ideas we have discussed here could represent a distinct component of social justice in future Scotland. One which takes account of how inequality affects both genders but also sees the Right to a meaningful role, through work, family or community life as inalienable. If this takes account of how both men and women have been denied inclusion and the opportunity 'to be somebody' then perhaps the components of the crisis of masculinity highlighted in this discussion will be some way to being addressed.

Guys, for the challenge, support and sharing of food.

Pete

2 OCTOBER 2013

When I started on this project I was convinced that masculinity was in *crisis*. My conviction was founded on my years of policing experience where I had come across hundreds of young men in *crisis* and their background and personal circumstances were often strikingly similar. Violence, alcohol, dysfunctional families, absent fathers and no work or even the prospect or aspiration of finding work were the key shared histories that were all too common to victims as well as perpetrators.

In the past few years I have been asking myself and others the question 'what is it be a man in 21st century Scotland?' I suspected lots of young men had no idea what being a man meant and I certainly didn't know and couldn't define it. I started thinking about the descriptors I would use to describe being a man and words like courage, integrity, loyalty were all I could come up with; I suspect the relevance of these words and what they mean in relation to being a man are literally out of date. To be honest they are words that I identify with personally but I appreciate they fall short of an accurate description of a 21st century man. So, I am still unsure.

When addressing conferences the response to this 'what is it to be a man?' question was always nodding heads in the audience and I'm sure the nodding was to acknowledge the validity of the question, no one volunteered an answer. This was the same response irrespective of audience gender, confirming for me that there was indeed a *crisis* and it was a *masculine crisis*. I also believed that one of principle reasons for this *crisis* was the changing role of men, in the home, the work place and society more generally. I considered this changing role was brought about in large part by the impact of feminism including the feminisation of the workforce and cited the absence of positive male role models in the home, in schools, in the work place as the supporting evidence for my conclusion. I knew the problem and I knew the cause and I even had an idea of the solution.

These discussions have made me rethink my conclusion. I was assuming I understood the problem, I was assuming I knew the main cause and I was assuming the solution to the problem was to be found in that cause. I was viewing feminism as the principle causal factor – this was incredibly simplistic, although I had to start somewhere. This view also pointed to a solution being found by addressing directly the impact that feminism was having on the role of men and this would evolve naturally out of an adversarial process of debate, creating a solution and of course in his process of debate entrenching the problem in the 'man' box and I expect too creating winners and losers. I hadn't considered that a more holistic and inclusive examination of the *crisis* affecting men might be a more fruitful and effective method of identifying solutions. Such a process requires the involvement of more than just men, it will involve women it will not be specific to a generation or even a class and it will undoubtedly uncover solutions that will be different for men and women but the outcomes will be shared and better for both sexes.

I've also confirmed that I do not currently possess the necessary mental furniture to allow me to articulate the *crisis* or to even properly understand it and identifying solutions seems way beyond my understanding and intellect. Perhaps my desire to fix a problem I cannot properly define using solutions that I cannot begin to imagine is not only arrogant but perhaps it's also a uniquely male thing.

Our connectedness as humans is vital to our wellbeing. We are born connected and relationships remain a constant theme throughout our human lives. From the mother/child, father/child relationship to how we treat the stranger on the street, these are things that mark us out as humans. Within these relationships our individual roles are also of immense importance not only for our personal wellbeing and happiness but also for the wellbeing and happiness of others in our circle. We are co-dependent and that's how it is, we are connected and that's how it is. The human model of connection and dependency has to be equal for it all to work well. It is by working harder to better understand the impact of the transition on our gender-based relationships that we will be most effective in defining the changing role of men and equally important the changing role of women.

Humans thrive when they have a 'sense of coherence' and so the experience of growing up in secure nurturing stable family circumstances is vitally important. It is for this reason that the role of men as father is crucial. My experience of young men in crisis suggests that fathers are usually absent from their lives or when present mostly have a negative impact. This then becomes a generational issue with negativity passing from one generation to the next.

Work is an important part of our personal stories but there has been a significant shift in the type of work available. There was an expectation that occupations were for life: men learned a trade and that is usually what they did for their entire working life. The column headed 'occupation' still requires to be completed on birth certificates and marriage certificates (I think) supporting our assumption that what we work at or how we earn our living is important and in some ways it defines us, whether we like it or not. Even if all we can enter in the occupation is 'labourer' it at least defines us as working; although do women use the term 'spinster' when they complete the marriage certificate?

It's as if we have assumed that all men could do was heavy industrial job, the sort of work that required strength and when these jobs 'disappeared' there was a great collective sigh of 'oh well, that's it for us'. Our resignation and acceptance of this false future was made worse by a social support system that allowed us to survive. Meanwhile women who were pushing for more equality including in the type of work available to them and took advantage of the opportunity. It's not that men couldn't do the new jobs it seems that we spent too long bemoaning the change and not 'managing the transition.'

I do believe that 'meaningful' work will be a crucial component of any solution providing as it does the opportunity for relationships beyond familial and providing men the sense of purpose, belonging and worth that is important to us all as humans. It is in the area of work, where the differences between the role of men compared to the role of women is most stark and which is used as a measure of equality and sometimes inequality. It is here therefore that any meaningful change may be apparent and where the shared challenge of equality can be most easily described and any areas of agreement and disagreement articulated.

I still believe that men face a challenge but I now believe that it is a challenge of coping better with the societal transitions and this affects everyone and it is a challenge that is not gender-specific nor confined to a single generation.

Thanks, it's been emotional!

John

2 OCTOBER 2013

Dear all,

This is great fun – but I want to end on a note of challenge. A bit of an epistle actually, so be warned. I'm not looking for a consensus just because we are closing, rather the opposite. I'm seeking out differences. That's not to say there is not a consensus emerging and Pete's last piece is a very reflective and intelligent example and John's last call for courage, integrity and loyalty I embrace wholeheartedly.

For me, looking back, the commonality of John and my views are not because we are of a similar generation. Nor is it because both John and I have both worked with boys who are 'at risk' – as the alarmingly revealing jargon calls them. Rather, I read Pete and David's contributions and see a difference in their perspectives that does not come from their younger years. I know many men in their 30s and 40s who would gravitate more to what John and I have been saying.

So, what is this difference? I will pick up on Pete first, and focus particularly on where he excellently summed up a feminist position that has been very familiar to me throughout my life. He said that 'Feminism was not only a movement which promoted the rights of women but was also in the vanguard of unpacking the idea of gender as an enactment, something we did rather than what we are, in which male and female play-off and define one another consciously and unconsciously'

I know that Pete said a lot more than this. However, I felt throughout our dialogue that this position lay at the heart of many of his responses. I imagine from Pete's last contribution that he is beginning to question that statement but nevertheless I feel the need to address it head on, because it is an all too common position held by many today – particularly amongst the formulators of social, education and health policy and interventions. Men as well as women. I will come to David's line of argument later.

Put to one side for a moment all the stats on gender imbalance and trends in crime, employment, pay, sexual assault, health and education. Similarly too, the long and often cruel history of power abuse that shaped these trends and has left a deep imprint on each genders' psyche. Indeed, in a moment of dream like madness – imagine it's all been solved.

When you strip it all back would we still be left with something definable as a uniquely male identity? Are there uniquely male characteristics that come from our biology and our genes? How does one shape the other? And is it true that we, all males, are united by a common imprint that will never change?

Does this process indeed create a way of being, psyche and brain functionality that is uniquely male? A pattern of behaviour and thought that is forever specific to our gender? Is this not the nub of the problem? Is there a level where men simply won't or can't change? Such a conclusion disquiets social engineering philosophies such as feminism and socialism, which seek equality through sameness – despite their protestations to the contrary.

For me the deep subtle, powerful and irritatingly-difficult-to-define unique male identity is real. Our brains are different. Our bodies are different. But it is more than that. Us boys, all of us, straight and gay, go the through the same three stages of change – different to girls. Changes which I believe unite us in a common unique experience that collectively shapes us.

The first is straight science. In the womb we all, male and female, start as XX, then we boys change from XX to XY. We begin the change – the move away. Girls don't. What's that got to do with anything? Well, mum's body goes to work to build a male child, not a female. But apart from that? Who can say for sure? Yet the difference exists, and the first change happens in the womb.

The second happens in infancy, when we start to move away from mum, when we get just how different from mum we really are. We won't grow up to be a big version of her. We are like dad – if he's around. It is a psychological process of differentiation that is exclusively male. For many it becomes a life-long battle to separate from mum.

Finally (in terms of guaranteed shared male-only experiences) there is puberty. Our hormones go wild, but all that happens on the surface is a voice change and a creeping hairiness. There's a bit of our anatomy that becomes a lot more important than it used to be. But we can't and will never be able to grow and give birth to another human being.

These 'changes' and their effects are of course debatable in terms of their real significance in the scheme of things. But they do happen only to us as males, so they must help to shape us. Not completely of course, but no matter how many dolls are thrown into the pram instead of guns, we as males will respond differently. We might well prefer the dolls, but we will do so as boys preferring dolls. We won't stop being boys.

There are other things that happen too. As very young boys we play together differently when with our own kind. We are noisier, we are more physical, we search for weakness and learn early on that avoiding being the runt of the litter is a crucial lesson in survival. Later on the taunt of being like a girl carries powerful traction. Boys – and later men – insult each other differently. We challenge and dare each other's boy-ness. And if it's not accusations of being like a girl – it is being gay.

Which brings me to David. His line from the beginning has been to question whether as a gay man he has actually experienced any crisis in masculinity – or whatever we are calling it now. He posed the question as to whether this was not a 'crisis in heterosexual male identity'. This thought has stayed with me throughout. I think it is not only an excellent question, but in my view actually comes very close to the nub of it all, but not in the way that David seems to imply.

It is interesting that none of the rest of us have seriously picked up on this core question from David. There has been a creeping consensus emerging since the sixties that if you are white, don't debate what it might be like to be black; if you are male, don't profess to know anything about womanhood; and if you are heterosexual don't comment on the gay experience. It is a 'ghetto-ist' position that separates us from our common humanity and our daily mixing and relating with that 'other'. An 'other' that we must never have a view on lest we offend and re-assert our white male heterosexual power domination.

I can bore you senseless on dogs. I know a lot about them – how their brains work and the difference between their socialising and genetic inheritance. I am not a dog – but I live with an Alsatian Collie cross called Tia who is my sole companion. Yet, despite my near total lack of canine characteristics, no one says I shouldn't know about them and discuss their nuances. A poor example perhaps but you get my drift.

I'm not gay either but I know something of the gay scene. Without going into details I know a bit of what I'm talking about. Gay men behave differently from lesbians, because they are men! In some ways they are more men than the heterosexual variety. They in fact prefer men.

In my early adult life I was a gardener for the council (Sheffield). It was an all-male 'Gang' (that was the official term) of eight. Redundant 30/40 something steel workers and 20 something lads into not much else other than Wednesday and the Blades. I was the youngest. Every day for three years there was at least one gay joke and countless gay innuendos. There was tonnes of physical contact, brawling, rough hugging, slapping, and play fighting. In the neighbouring Gang there were at least two openly gay men – well known thugs in the Sheffield United crew (the Blades – unless you hadn't worked that one out). The rest of us (myself included) were at pains to demonstrate that we were not ourselves gay and kept our inner doubts to ourselves.

The times they may be a-changing but in my generation (and I suspect still many others after) nearly all heterosexual men grow up with the same question. How do we connect with feelings of friendship, bonding and intimacy with other men? Heterosexual men know only too well the potential and imagined dreaded threat of the Gay label in our lives. No – I have seen too many men of my years struggle with their hidden sexual selves to buy into the notion that gay men are somehow outside of this debate.

So, now let's turn the other way. We as men live in a world with women, who are equally unique when you strip all the social engineering and historical power stuff away. These are the ones we need to get on with day-to-day – whether we are gay or straight.

We are living in times of breath-taking change on all fronts. To even try to list them is banal. A world in which the rich countries keep adult men away from children, especially in school, and one where gang rape, stoning and enforced female circumcision hit the world news, but don't go away.

Closer to home the political contradictions are bizarre. The 'rump UK' cabinet is almost a caricature of male elite club-ery, yet has legalised, indeed championed, gay marriage. Meanwhile the most macho part of the 'wider UK' is on course for a female First/Prime Minster after Salmond – Labour or SNP. And on the wider European stage we are led by a woman with a very different style of doing things, the amazing Angela Merkel – the most powerful woman in the world.

Nevertheless, I believe that at the heart of men there is a dark hate that is so horrific, we do not want to understand it but would rather imagine we can legislate and regulate it away. The torture, the rapes, the napalm bombings, are all universally carried out by men. There seems to be something in us men that can objectify the other and make us fit the cruelty spec perfectly. My own thesis is that this has something to do with our urgent need to separate in fundamentally different ways to girls when young (see above). Of course much of this evil has been coerced and encouraged by history where we as men held sway, and now that we are beginning to live in different times we hope that we can reduce its carnage. Perhaps we will, but we will never eliminate it. It lies dormant and little understood in our natures.

We cannot solve a problem by locating it only in one place. Hate, anger, rage, indeed even violence, are part of our mammal condition. Recently I witnessed a mother swan protecting her young by beating a seagull literally to death with her fierce wings. The seagull got the message pretty quick. It didn't need to die – but it was beaten continuously so ferociously until there was not a movement left in it.

Women are not swans and we are not seagulls, and indeed the maternal protective instinct is the usual caveat for murderous rage in women. The thing is that women can give vent to their anger, their rage, and their total conviction that by defeating the other they are making the world a better place. They can plot, enact vengeance, kill, collude and manipulate to win and satisfy their ends to awesome effect. To deny that potential in woman-kind is indeed misogynistic. Worship of innate female 'goodness' as a given is an integral component of the worst kind of patriarchy. But more than that women can use power in government as they have and are showing. Coming out of centuries of abuse against women we are now left grappling with women professionals' use of power to stamp out that dark potential in men so no women suffer as their forebears did. And I don't blame them. The historical balance sheet is grotesque. But the time is now for good men – in John's words, courageous, integral and loyal men, to step up to plate and help 'engineer' some balance.

So I sign off with a quote from a 60-year-old very feminist-influenced female psychotherapist friend of mine. In many ways it sums up my whole argument.

'If we only see the dark, hateful and rageful side of humanity in men, and men only, then we condemn women's dark side to go underground and become quietly yet effectively subversive.'

Indeed it has been great. Best to all. And thanks Gerry for creating this space.

Sandy

4 OCTOBER 2013

Dear all,

Forgive my tardiness – once again the demands of work, mainly party conference season, has interfered with my contributions to this (as ever) fascinating discussion.

I've enjoyed it, which might surprise Gerry as he may have detected a little reluctance on my part right at the beginning, but over time I began to see the point of it: an examination of the thesis (that there is a crisis in Scottish masculinity), a discussion sparked by that thesis (often wide ranging and sometimes well off the main point), then something approaching a conclusion. Have we achieved the third? Not really, but I'm not sure it matters very much.

I remain a sceptic, though I'm humbled by the extent to which John, Pete and Sandy have all considered the various themes that have come up – you've all clearly thought about it much more deeply than me, and while I don't disagree with a lot of your concluding observations, I still can't help feeling what we've been talking about goes well beyond gender and sexuality but is a crisis of humankind for all sorts of obvious reasons. Sure, this has a 'male' dimension, and perhaps even a distinct 'male' impact, but the solution – if any – is nothing less than a whole-scale transformation of Scottish/British society covering the economy, education, opportunity and, of course, work. Work, I think we can all agree, is pretty damn important.

Sandy's concluding thoughts I found particularly thought-provoking. And he's right, gay men do behave differently from gay women (at least in my and his experience). I have no lesbian friends and often don't really know how to engage with them (obviously a personal failing, don't get me wrong), and the two worlds don't often collide. If I'm being honest I prefer male company, though not exclusively so (I'm seeing a long-term female friend for lunch the day after I write this); gay friends of mine can't bring themselves to be too intimate with women because they think it's a waste of time. And while talking openly about gay stuff – as I discovered at the Labour and Conservative Party conferences (even though they took place in Brighton and Manchester respectively) – still causes my straight acquaintances a degree of discomfort, I still prefer their company. Women are much better at taking this on board, which makes my preference for male friendships all the stranger. I'd like to think my motivations aren't purely sexual! One good friend of mine, for example, is straight but loves talking to me about gay sex. Make of that what you will, although it does hint at the bond Sandy describes.

Just as an aside, I had an interesting experience the other day which merits airing before we call it a day. I was applying (online) for a minor public appointment, to serve on the board of a long-running Edinburgh-based Scottish institution. There was the usual equal opportunities stuff and I checked 'gay male' without really thinking about it. Later, when I was discussing the application with a (gay) government lawyer friend, he mentioned that a recent (and I assume internal) survey had shown that in general terms Scottish gay men preferred to check 'rather not say' or lie than admit to being gay whereas, by contrast, similar exercises in London result in a far higher degree of honesty. Perhaps that's not so surprising, indeed my friend said 'oh, it's because you live in London' (although I took issue with that), but it does point to a distinctly Scottish phenomenon, and one that might be linked to 'maleness'.

So, where do we take things from here? I'm not altogether sure, although this discussion has – at least – served to make me more conscious of gender and its importance in all sorts of areas, so I regard that as useful. Like Sandy I endorse John's plea for courage, integrity and loyalty.

It's been fun guys.

David

Observations by a Group of Women

Observations

TWELVE WOMEN OF various ages, backgrounds and professions were asked to give their views of the challenges facing men – Scottish men in particular – and if they thought men should and could change. Extracts from their anonymous answers that convey a variety of insights, positive and negative, appear below, followed by responses from the men who attempt to address some of the most salient points.

Firstly, when asked: 'what do they see as the main issues facing Scottish men in the 21st century?' One woman said, 'The biggest issue is the need for men to cede control and power to create equality'. They went on state that when children arrive many 'well paid men in decent relationships' don't rise to the occasion: 'They drink, they follow football, they indulge in their hobbies, they remove themselves emotionally, they cannot cope with the jealousy, they spend money on themselves before their families and they fornicate'.

Another noted the pressures on men as they 'face the saturation of the media with images of women to which men are expected to respond sexually while, simultaneously, the media also demands that men be anti-sexist, with the shaming of Savile and similar celebrities'. A further perspective addressed the changing economic times: 'Many men I know have been made redundant and although their wives work it has left them feeling that they have failed and unsure of what role/status/identity the now have'.

One made the challenging observation that, 'Scottish men tend to be more sexist than their English and American counterparts. Sexual relationships are still seen, at certain levels, as a power struggle'. A football fan and Tartan Army supporter got into the whole thorny issue of men and the game, reflecting that they 'wonder why the very same men who will behave impeccably at Scotland games will behave badly at Rangers/Celtic games. I've tried to look at what's different: they still drink as much (maybe more at Scotland)'.

Another woman viewed that, 'Young Scottish men have an unhealthy alcohol culture – the only way to have a good time is to get smashed at the weekend. And an unhealthy internet porn culture. Scottish men eat badly, smoke, don't exercise and are reluctant to visit a doctor' at the same time, 'Women are still badly represented in the boardroom, in politics and our major institutions. Old boy networks have far too much influence'. A challenging view from one woman, 'In a sexually 'equal' world, where the 'soft' people skills of women are more valued than traditional male strengths… what are men actually FOR?'

Secondly, they were asked whether there any uniquely or predominantly Scottish challenges facing men. This brought forth a range of views addressing the scale of change in industry, employment and jobs. One stated, 'Scottish masculinity, especially in the Central Belt of Scotland, was so tied to particular types of employment – coalmining, shipbuilding, trades, steel – historically that it was easy to 'be a man''. They continued: 'The death of these industries has had a terrible effect on Scottish men. Our young men have not moved beyond the culture of hard-drinking, fighting masculinity, but there is no longer employment for them where they can be protected, controlled and mentored into that culture'.

Thirdly, they were asked whether there was a crisis of Scottish men and masculinities. There were a range of opinions expressed with more agreement that there was a specific crisis, than not. One commented that there is a crisis, 'Yes. Evident on all the stats. Domestic abuse on the rise, unhealthy relationships even among the very young. Alcohol and substance misuse. Drunk and violent crime on nights out'.

Another stated that, 'Our young men are killing themselves in disproportionate numbers, with many more on the streets drunk and drugged with knives and weapons, utterly reckless about their own survival or that of others'. They went on, 'The homicide statistics are a depressing reflection of the crisis of modern Scottish masculinity – so many young men killed by their 'friends' and acquaintances over minor, drunken quarrels.'

One woman addressed one of the key questions of any 20-something or 30-something man, namely, 'What self-respecting Scottish bloke would want to be a 'new man'?' From a very different viewpoint, another stated that, 'Scottish masculinities still seem pretty two-dimensional: hard men or 'poofs''.

Two of the younger women, in their early 20s, questioned the idea of a crisis, one viewing that, 'I believe the concept of a crisis in masculinity is dangerous, and to be avoided. It implies that the small changes taking place in womens' status in society... are causing widespread psychological confusion among men.' The other stated, 'I can't comment on a crisis. Masculinity is perhaps more strictly defined in Scotland than other places'.

The last question was on what, if anything, should be a top priority of change. One perspective commented on the need for societal change:

> It is my sense that the social structures, cultural norms and workplace inequalities which demonstrably still undermine and undervalue women in Scotland today may actually limit the life experiences of men also, even as they give them unfair advantage in work environments etc.

Another from a mother-of-two stated that, 'We need to strip away the feminisation of our education system'. Reflecting on her experience of bringing up two boys ten years apart, and years of them being ticked off or viewed unmanageable, felt this was all for, 'Simply for being boys and for the women in charge not having a clue how to harness all that energy and age appropriate 'boyness' effectively'.

As an even more direct call on men to change their behaviour and men to take responsibility for the actions of other men, one stated, 'Men must call each other out on sexism and misogyny. They need to name sexism when they see it, especially in the workplace'. She reflected on her own experience in work and politics, 'I am sick to death of Lefty men who talk a good game but rarely back it up with actions'.

There was an undoubted anger in some of the women's contributions and many will say this is understandable given the nature of society, inequalities between men and women, and the behaviour of some men. We now turn back to the four who respond on turn to these comments in a final set of observations.

David, John, Pete and Sandy's replies

DAVID'S RESPONSE

WHILE THE FEEDBACK is, as one would expect, varied and often thoughtful, I couldn't help feeling some parts verged on caricature. Several comment painted a picture of Scottish men indulging in an orgy of sex, booze and violence that I don't really recognise (although Glasgow on a Friday night certainly looks that way). Of course it's true in some respects, but hardly a blanket phenomenon.

One said the 'biggest issue is the need for men to cede control and power to create equality', which is undoubtedly true, although some acknowledgement of the power and control already ceded might have made the observation more balanced. I got the impression that a few of the assessments were stuck in the 1980s. 'They drink, they follow football, they indulge in their hobbies,' said another, 'they remove themselves emotionally, they cannot cope with the jealousy, they spend money on themselves before their families and they fornicate.' It's a very hostile view of Scottish men that would be considered offensive if applied in reverse (i.e. Scottish men talking about women).

One comment makes the perfectly reasonable observation that the decline of heavy industry in the 1980s was difficult for traditional concepts of Scottish masculinity, which is undoubtedly true, but I still can't help feeling it's a bit out of date. Even by the early 1990s the Scottish economy had changed significantly, pushing men into different occupations – many better paid and certainly safer than the old – while also liberating many Scottish women from poorly-paid factory work (and indeed not working at all). Again this is a generalisation, but the picture is not as black-and-white as some of the comments appear to suggest. 'Our young men have not moved beyond the culture of hard-drinking, fighting masculinity' was another comment. Really? 'Scottish men eat badly, smoke, don't exercise and are reluctant to visit a doctor'. I don't have the stats to hand, but the explosion in gym membership (if not use), healthy eating, sports, etc. would all suggest otherwise, while anecdotally it doesn't chime with my personal background experience, which isn't exactly a standard middle class one.

'Scottish masculinities still seem pretty two-dimensional,' said another, 'hard men or 'poofs''. Again, really? Public attitudes towards homosexuality have shifted dramatically, while there's strong evidence among younger age groups that it's barely an issue at all so normalised has it become. I agree with the person who said that men 'must call each other out on sexism and misogyny. They need to name sexism when they see it, especially in the workplace', and particularly liked her supplementary remark about being 'sick to death of Lefty men who talk a good game but rarely back it up with actions'. A good point, although I still think the situation in the early 21st century is unquestionably better than in the 1980s, which again is where I feel a lot of these observations belong. Sure, a lot could still be changed, tackled and improved, but it's always useful to acknowledge already significant progress.

David

JOHN'S RESPONSE

Some interesting responses and maybe typical of our *Scottishness*, I'm right you're wrong, I'm better and that's it, case made and if you're not happy, sod off.

The word equality peppers most discussions about gender but even a cursory look behind the words suggests that for many women 'equality' is founded on the premise that women can do everything men can do and better, but men are hopeless and cannot do what women do, '...what are men FOR?' The responses confirm this simplistic view.

It seems that employment is becoming the primary measure of value in relation to status and so it seems the battle that women wage for equality is usually fought in boardrooms with glass ceilings. One of the respondents suggests that the 'crisis' for men is likely a result of this loss of status that has left them unsure of their role, again making the direct link to employment. There is an inherent danger that by concentrating discussion of gender inequality on paid employment we are devaluing the unpaid roles all of us fulfill in society. If a father takes his child to nursery the mothers, and even the staff, 99 per cent female, will ask if he's 'babysitting' confirming the belief that fathers don't have a defined parenting role, except perhaps as a substitute for mum, the real parent and principal care giver. So if he's not out working and earning money, everything else he does is irrelevant.

I often ask women why more men are not nursery teachers or doctors' receptionists and the response is usually that these jobs don't pay enough. This may or may not be true but it does not explain the imbalance in teaching, where there is no disparity in status or salary. I'm not sure of the numbers but I think too there is an increasing gender imbalance in promoted posts within teaching; this should be expected when the majority of the eligible candidates are women. (I'm using imbalance instead of unequal, not sure why?)

I suppose that living in a world that values commodity above community, and where success is measured by how much we earn and how many things we own, the focus on earnings should not be a surprise. Neither should it be unexpected that women view success in this area as important, it is important, but it's not the only measure of equality.

I don't think increasing the pay for receptionists or cleaners or nursery teachers would see a flood of male applicants for these jobs. The pay for these jobs reflects the value we place on them.

If *Equality* is what we all really want and strive for in every facet of our society, not least because of the negative impact of inequality, then we need to all agree what it is we value. Currently people who make most money get the biggest rewards. We haven't so far valued the role of women, at least that role men are incapable of fulfilling, as a mother. It's also true that we haven't so far valued the role of father either. Perhaps an interesting thought experiment might be to produce a job description and person specification for each role, then evaluate the salary scale and would there be a bonus scheme, or a pension entitlement?

What I find most interesting and encouraging too, is the obvious difference that age appears to have on the notion of masculinity in crisis. It seems younger women don't recognise any significant challenge. This generational contrast is also reflected in our exchanges. Sandy and I have seen more change therefore we are a little less relaxed about it, in general. The idea of human evolution holds true for everyone, it's meant to be like this therefore how we manage transition is key.

Whether we believe as individuals that there is a crisis that solely inflicts men is in many respects less important than the belief that there is a crisis that affects everyone and it is fundamentally one of *Equality* and it should be a matter of real concern to us all. I know that not all women want a professional career and are more than fulfilled being a mum. Would they define that role as being in crisis?

Our discussions have been about masculinity and I remain struck by David's suggestion during our exchanges that men are not coping as well with transition as women.

Our current societal compass heading seems to be that we strive relentlessly to get as much as we can for ourselves and anything that appears to hinder progress towards that goal must be removed. Accepting that change is inevitable could we at least agree a common purpose and that will be to create more *Equal* society, for everyone.

John

PETE'S RESPONSE

The identification of the challenges facing Scottish men and what needs to change in the women's responses were familiar. They have a difficult truth to them and some we raise in our discussion, but perhaps do not solve. I can't help but see 'the problem with men' as part of a bigger problem around the unequal distribution of respect and prestige in society, and not just in Scotland. The apparent redundancy of men is not entirely their fault. Their failure to adapt, to invent new versions of themselves more fitting of the times, needs to be understood within a context of powerlessness that many men experience today.

I question the extent to which the problems identified are solely to do with gender in isolation from other forms of power and powerlessness. Throughout the conversation, I have been advocating an analysis of 'the problem with men' in terms of a loss of role, a loss of usefulness which stems not from the biological or psychological traits of a particular gender (if such things could be said to exist) but a process which has made the powerless of men *and women* starker than ever. Sometimes we look at the reasons why women underperform, sometimes we look at why men fail or come up short as human beings. Never in serious debates are women blamed for the problems associated with their gender. I suggest, for the time being, we afford men the same freedom from blame. Except in the instances of interpersonal violence or abuse of women by men, I also wonder how helpful it is to blame one gender for the problems of the other. This works for men's challenges too and I resist the idea that these can be blamed on the (relative) success of feminism. Far from it, feminism is the great lost opportunity for men. Responding to an offer to construct other forms of masculinity, of reimagining other forms of relationships between the genders, I hope, is a stalled project rather than an abandoned one. Women as well as men have a role here. 'What self-respecting Scottish bloke would want to be a 'new man?'"; take care around what possible genders we construct for each other.

That 'the biggest issue is the need for men to cede control and power and create equality' misses my point. The failure to produce a more just and equal society cannot be laid at the feet of men, all men, as a gender block. For many men (and women), self-respect and the ability to follow a life which is rewarding and empowering has been denied them. Ceding power and control depends on having these at your disposal in the first place. The problem for many people living in Scotland is they lack the power to author their own lives, to feel good about who they are and to look into the mirror of other people's success and be assured they 'count'.

Gender is of course a dimension of these everyday injuries of inequality. The fragility of our relationships are the cost of an increasingly depersonalised and materialistic public life; the more material our society, the more hollowed out our emotional and interpersonal experiences. Those men who 'drink, follow football, indulge in their hobbies, remove themselves emotionally, cannot cope with jealousy, spend money on themselves before their families and fornicate.' Are they happy? Is this a sign of their power or powerlessness? Who, given the best of all possible conditions and the power and freedom to construct an ideal life, would choose this?

The absence of a sense of belonging was a theme I left our conversation with. My own approach to insulate myself from the challenges of the gender debate, to distance myself from the crimes of men, particularly the violent aspects, has been operationalising the 'I' over the 'we'. If looking for groups to belong to, the Y chromosome never had an attractive enough flag for me to rally around. Belonging to a group called 'men' does not appeal to my individualist instincts but I have been challenged by these conversations to now see these instincts as my loss.

I have also tried to resist the Scottish dimension of the conversation, which crops up in the women's responses (prompted, admittedly). Perhaps in part because I'm English but also because I honestly believe there is no Scottish exceptionalism evident in the harms to self and others, loss of role, identity and meaning that face Scottish men. It may be harder to enact a different type of masculinity in Scotland, but I don't know if this is true.

It's certainly harder to be the type of adult young men could once learn to be. One where you could leave school with relatively modest qualifications and find employment that offered the prospect of growing skills, wages and prestige over time. Growth that would lay the foundations, start a family independently of the state or parents, stand up in a community and 'count', to be respected and have the confidence to respect others. Opportunity has become pornographic for many young men; images of unrealistic acts of conspicuous consumption stripped of the real relationships of life. So, yes, woman are denied their full potential in the world of work, held back by glass ceilings and old boy networks, but let's remember that these exclude many young men too and the psychic and physical cost on many of these young men has been great in recent times. There needs to be roles for all and we can all help, by identifying what exactly it is about men that is valued and by supporting a variety of roles for men and women to fill.

It is here that I believe Scotland has a better chance than other places. In part because of its greater reluctance to hurtle along the neo-liberal path and its relative community mindedness. But we must beware, the strength of collectivism is a commitment to fairness but it can also single out the new and different, the outsider, as suspicious and morally questionable with the potential to undermine the cherished collectivity. The vanguard of the new masculinities may come from the gay community, the 'new men', those choosing or adapting to childlessness, or a myriad of other places outside the consensus.

I wholeheartedly believe men have to change and new versions of masculinity need to be negotiated. Men can help each other with this, by pulling each other up on gender speech in the same way as is now common with ethnicity. But it does not begin and end with men and how we frame the problem of men will determine the depth of societal self–reflection required.

Pete

SANDY'S RESPONSE

It can be very emotive when men and women collectively exchange views on the other's gender. Generalisations sweep all before them. Defensiveness and blame fills the air. Hardly surprising, really. Men and women hurt each other constantly. In our families and relationships, the other gender is usually there witnessing or contributing to our emotional vulnerability and weaknesses. Husbands, wives, partners, parents, children and siblings; they all play their part in our hurts, as well as being the ones we can't help but love, and need.

So, it was with sadness, but no real surprise, that I read some of the comments from this selection of women. Sadness, not just because I've heard some such comments many times before, but because their grievances will never be satisfied. As long as dads are dads there will be those who absent themselves when the child is born, struggling (or not) to hide their jealousy. And when does any group (especially one making up 50 per cent of the population) organise itself across generations to consciously cede control and power in some kind of undefined collective way? And as for the behaviour stuff. Personally I've got absolutely no intension of crushing my passion for football, giving up drink, or suppressing my hobbies – and nor do almost all the men I know (thank God). That is so not the problem!

It sometimes feels like the unattractive traits in humanity – selfishness, infidelity, meanness, and emotional absence – have become per se 'male traits'. (Which of course implies that women, in an equally general sense, do not cheat, lie or act selfishly.) I may be imagining this, but it read as if there was not much liking of men coming through in these comments. It seems we are either to be blamed for hanging on to power and behaving 'badly' across the board, or we are to be pitied because we fight each other, think too much about sex, and eat the wrong food. But little in the way of empathy.

We do have a problem between the genders. Running parallel to the gobsmacking pace of change over the past half century that has significantly (and I would argue, permanently) changed the balance of gender power in the western world, there are still way too many acts of unspeakable cruelty meted out against women by men in conscious gender hatred. But behind the horror headlines, many decent men are left struggling to find their place in the new world unfolding, scorched of the comforting, yet constricting, totems of the past. Many also quietly ask that same question to themselves – what are we as men actually for? (Isn't this the saddest of questions?) Many more don't know what proof of manhood actually means – beyond drink, sex and fighting. All too often amongst our young men the message preached is of excess in all quarters as the surest route to real-man credibility. Rarely spoken about or encouraged in a consciously male way are the qualities of courage, loyalty, duty and love. Yet they are there, overtly or subtly, in action rather than words, in the everyday lives of many men.

My fundamental point in the contributions enclosed is not to strive for men to be more like women, but rather to support men to be good men. Not by copying or being led by women, but by finding a man's way to do noble and life affirming stuff. I just hope that in the meantime there aren't too many women banking on an all-or-nothing conversion of Scottish men to sobriety, healthy eating, 'soft skills' and anti-sexist vigilance. Because it won't happen, never will, nor should it. Each gender has its purpose, its genetics, its own different way of being – in kindness and in hate. There will always be things about the other gender that annoy us. Always! But for each person, our gender and our sexuality are formative currents in the shaping of who we are, and to be celebrated. They are not to be averaged, even equalised, out of existence. *Vivé la difference!*

Sandy

Some other books published by **LUATH** PRESS

Caledonian Dreaming: The Quest for a Different Scotland

Gerry Hassan
ISBN: 978-1-910021-32-3 PBK £11.99

 *Caledonian Dreaming: The Quest for a Different Scotland* offers a penetrating and original way forward for Scotland beyond the current independence debate.

It identifies the myths of modern Scotland, describes what they say and why they need to be seen as myths. Hassan argues that Scotland is already changing, as traditional institutions and power decline and new forces emerge, and outlines a prospectus for Scotland to become more democratic and to embrace radical and far-reaching change.

Hassan drills down to deeper reasons why the many dysfunctions of British democracy could dog an independent Scotland too. With a non-partisan but beady eye on society both sides of the border, in this clever book here are tougher questions to consider than a mere Yes/No

POLLY TOYNBEE writer and journalist, The Guardian

A brilliant book unpacking the political narratives that have shaped modern Scotland in order to create a space to imagine anew. A book about Scotland important to anyone, anywhere, dreaming a new world.

STEPHEN DUNCOMBE, author

There could be no better harbinger of [...] possibilities than this bracing, searching, discomfiting and ultimately exhilarating book.

FINTAN O'TOOLE

Glass Half Full: Moving Beyond Scottish Miserabilism

Eleanor Yule and David Manderson
ISBN: 978-1-910021-34-7 PBK £7.99

 A self-help book for the Scottish psyche

Cultural Miserabilism: the power of the negative story with no redemption and no escape, that wallows in its own bleakness.

Scotland is a small and immensely creative country. The role of the arts and culture is one that many are rightly proud of. But do we portray Scotland in the light we should?

There is a tendency in film, literature and other cultural output to portray the negative aspects of Scottish life. In *Seeing Ourselves*, filmmaker Eleanor Yule and academic David Manderson explore the origins of this bleak take on Scottish life, its literary and cultural expressions, and how this phenomenon in film has risen to the level of a genre which audiences both domestic and international see as a recognisable story of contemporary Scotland.

What does miserabilism tell us about ourselves? When did we become cultural victims? Is it time we move away from an image of Scotland that constantly casts itself as the poor relation?

From the *Trainspotting* to the Kailyard, Seeing Ourselves confronts the negative Scotland we portray not only to the world but, most importantly, ourselves.

Do [they] accurately reflect the reality of life in Scotland for the majority of the population or are they just 'stories' we like to tell ourselves about ourselves?

ELEANOR YULE

Blossom: What Scotland Needs to Flourish

Lesley Riddoch
ISBN: 978-1-908373-69-4 PBK £11.99

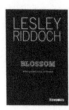

Weeding out vital components of Scottish identity from decades of political and social tangle is no mean task, but it's one journalist Lesley Riddoch has undertaken.

Dispensing with the tired, yo-yoing jousts over fiscal commissions, devo something-or-other and EU in-or-out, Blossom pinpoints both the buds of growth and the blight that's holding Scotland back. Drawing from its people and history, as well as the experience of the Nordic countries and the author's own passionate and outspoken perspective, this is a plain-speaking but incisive call to restore equality and control to local communities and let Scotland flourish.

Not so much an intervention in the independence debate as a heartfelt manifesto for a better democracy.
THE SCOTSMAN

Scotland: A Suitable Case for Treatment

Tom Brown and Henry McLeish
ISBN: 978-1-906307-69-1 PBK £9.99

Joining forces again to attack the political establishment, Tom Brown and Henry McLeish embark on a comprehensive examination of the ailments ravaging Scotland and the Union. The diagnosis? That the Scots are a schizophrenic people in crisis whose internal tumult has been writ large on recent British politics. What is called for is radical change, for a 'new politics', for a more confident nation that can bury the hatchet with England and stand alone as a leader in a global world.

Notes from the North

Emma Wood
ISBN 1 84282 048 6 PBK £7.99

Notes from the North is a pragmatic, positive and forward-looking contribution to cultural and political debate within Scotland.

- Notes on being English
- Notes on being in Scotland
- Learning from a shared past

Sickened by the English jingoism that surfaced in rampant form during the 1982 Falklands War, Emma Wood started to dream of moving from her home in East Anglia to the Highlands of Scotland. She felt increasingly frustrated and marginalised as Thatcherism got a grip on the southern English psyche. The Scots she met on frequent holidays in the Highlands had no truck with Thatcherism, and she felt at home with grass-roots Scottish anti-authoritarianism. The decision was made. She uprooted and headed for a new life in the north of Scotland.

In this book she sets a study of Scots-English conflicts alongside relevant personal experiences of contemporary incomers' lives in the Highlands. She was to discover that she had crossed a border in more than the geographical sense. Her own approach has been thoughtful and creative.

This is an intelligent and perceptive book. It is calm, reflective, witty and sensitive about an issue which can sometimes generate more heat than light. ...it should...be read by all Scots concerned about what kind of nation we live in. They might learn something about themselves.
THE HERALD

Singin I'm No a Billy He's a Tim

Des Dillon
ISBN 978 1 908373 05 2 PBK £6.99

What happens when you lock up a Celtic fan?

What happens when you lock up a Celtic fan with a Rangers fan?

What happens when you lock up a Celtic fan with a Rangers fan on the day of the Old Firm match?

Des Dillon watches the sparks fly as Billy and Tim clash in a rage of sectarianism and deep-seated hatred. When children have been steeped in bigotry since birth, is it possible for them to change their views?

Join Billy and Tim on their journey of discovery. Are you singing their tune?

Explosive.
EVENING NEWS

His raucous sense of humour and keen understanding of the west-coast sectarian mindset make his sisters-under-the-skin message seem a matter of urgency and not just a liberal platitude.
THE GUARDIAN

The sheer vitality of the theatrical writing – the seamless combination of verbal wit and raw kinetic energy, and the pure dynamic strength of the play's structure – makes [Singin I'm No a Billy He's a Tim] *feel like one of the shortest and most gripping two-hour shows in current Scottish theatre.*
THE SCOTSMAN

This Road is Red

Alison Irvine

ISBN 978 1906817 81 7 PBK £7.99

It is 1964. Red Road is rising out of the fields. To the families who move in, it is a dream and a shining future.

It is 2010. The Red Road Flats are scheduled for demolition. Inhabited only by intrepid asylum seekers and a few stubborn locals, the once vibrant scheme is tired and out of time.

Between these dates are the people who filled the flats with laughter, life and drama. Their stories are linked by the buildings; the sway and buffet of the tower blocks in the wind, the creaky lifts, the views and the vertigo. *This Road is Red* is a riveting and subtle novel of Glasgow.

One of the most important books about Glasgow and urban life I've read in a very long time. It offers an insight into city life that few Scottish novels can emulate.
PROFESSOR WILLY MALEY

Trackman

Catriona Child

ISBN: 978-1-908373-43-4 PBK £7.99

Trackman Trackman Trackman Trackman Trackman Trackman Trackman

Davie was about to leave the MP3 player lying on the pavement when something stopped him. A voice in his head.

You'll regret it if you leave it. You'll only come back for it later.

Can a song change your life?

Can a song bring people, places and moments in time alive again?

Davie Watts is the Trackman. He knows what song to play to you and he knows exactly when you need to hear it. Davie seeks out strangers in need and helps them using the power of music.

The Girl on the Ferryboat
Angus Peter Campbell
ISBN 978 1 908373 77 9 HBK £12.99

'Sorry,' I said to her, trying to stand to one side, and she smiled and said, 'O, don't worry – I'll get by.'

They say it is the things in life that you don't do that you regret. For Alasdair and Helen, a chance encounter on the ferry from Oban to Mull leads to a lifetime of wondering what might have been.

This vividly evoked novel is a mirage of memories; a tale of love, loss and regret woven around that single, momentous meeting on a ferryboat one summer.

I have no doubts that Angus Peter Campbell is one of the few really significant living poets in Scotland, writing in any language.
SORLEY MACLEAN

Angus Peter Campbell has a very considerable gift indeed.
NORMAN MACCAIG

Extraordinary imaginative writing.
THE INDEPENDENT

Da Happie Laand
Robert Alan Jamieson
ISBN 978 1906817 86 2 PBK £9.99

In the summer of the year of the Millennium, a barefoot stranger comes to the door of the manse for help. But three days later he disappears without trace, leaving a bundle of papers behind.

Da Happie Laand weaves the old minister's attempt to make sense of the mysteries left behind by his 'lost sheep' – the strange tale of a search for his missing father at midsummer – with an older story relating the fate of a Zetlandic community across the centuries, the tales of those people who emigrated to New Zetland in the South Pacific, and those who stayed behind.

Jamieson's strange masterpiece Da Happie Laand *haunts dreams and waking hours, as it takes my adopted home of Shetland, twisting it and the archipelago's history into the most disturbing, amazing, slyly funny shapes.*

TOM MORTON, *The Sunday Herald*

Details of these and other books published by Luath Press can be found at:
www.luath.co.uk

Luath Press Limited

committed to publishing well written books worth reading

LUATH PRESS takes its name from Robert Burns, whose little collie Luath (*Gael.,* swift or nimble) tripped up Jean Armour at a wedding and gave him the chance to speak to the woman who was to be his wife and the abiding love of his life. Burns called one of 'The Twa Dogs' Luath after Cuchullin's hunting dog in Ossian's *Fingal*. Luath Press was established in 1981 in the heart of Burns country, and now resides a few steps up the road from Burns' first lodgings on Edinburgh's Royal Mile.

Luath offers you distinctive writing with a hint of unexpected pleasures.

Most bookshops in the UK, the US, Canada, Australia, New Zealand and parts of Europe either carry our books in stock or can order them for you. To order direct from us, please send a £sterling cheque, postal order, international money order or your credit card details (number, address of cardholder and expiry date) to us at the address below. Please add post and packing as follows: UK – £1.00 per delivery address; overseas surface mail – £2.50 per delivery address; overseas airmail – £3.50 for the first book to each delivery address, plus £1.00 for each additional book by airmail to the same address. If your order is a gift, we will happily enclose your card or message at no extra charge.

Luath Press Limited
543/2 Castlehill
The Royal Mile
Edinburgh EH1 2ND
Scotland
Telephone: 0131 225 4326 (24 hours)
Fax: 0131 225 4324
email: sales@luath.co.uk
Website: www.luath.co.uk